ADVENTURES ON FOOT & BY WATER IN
THE WYE VALLEY & THE FOREST OF DEAN

FOREST
DIARIES

DEBORAH FERNEYHOUGH-SWEET

ADVENTURES ON FOOT & BY WATER IN
THE WYE VALLEY & THE FOREST OF DEAN

FOREST
DIARIES

MEMOIRS
Cirencester

Published by Memoirs

MEMOIRS
PUBLISHING

25 Market Place, Cirencester, Gloucestershire, GL7 2NX
info@memoirsbooks.co.uk www.memoirspublishing.com

First published in England, March 2013

Book jacket design Ray Lipscombe

ISBN 978-1-909544-38-3

Printed in England

This book is dedicated to my father-in-law,
Leonard Sidney Ferneyhough,
a Monmouthshire man: April 1929 - March 2008.

CONTENTS

ABOUT THE AUTHOR

Deborah Ferneyhough-Sweet was born in Tewkesbury, Gloucestershire on December 26th 1958 to Donald and Barbara Sweet. Her father was a member of the well-respected firm B Sweet & Sons Undertakers. Deborah is married to Charles Ferneyhough, and they have three-grown up children. A keen canoeist and woodland walker, she has been visiting the Forest of Dean since she was 16 years old. Photography, writing, and poetry relating to the place she loves the most, the Forest of Dean, are her passions.

The need to always be here,
and the passion that never leaves my heart.
To get in my canoe, and feel its river.
To walk through its forest, to breathe and feel its existence,
To grow with it, when I am dust.

LEARNING
THE RIVER

～

SUMMER 1999

I was born in the river town of Tewkesbury, so I was always surrounded by water. My father told me how he had learned to swim as a boy in the River Avon, as many of his generation did before the war.

In the summer of 1999 my children were still young, and I had always wanted to take them canoeing. I had been coming to the Forest of Dean since I was sixteen, and continued to do so when I had the children. We had gone for long walks with them here since they had been in their prams, so now I felt brave enough to take them to the waters of the River Wye.

We hired a canoe for the day at Symonds Yat, receiving briefing instructions on how to paddle a canoe. As we drifted away from land, I remember how frightened the children were. The canoe rocked unsteadily at any slight movement, and everyone knows how fidgety children can be. This did nothing for my new-found confidence in the safety of canoeing - perhaps I had bitten more off than I could chew.

Paddling upriver was hard work, specially as we were doing it for the first time. The expanse of the river looked so wide that I felt as if it was going to swallow us up. But I knew somehow that I was made for canoeing, because when I began to enjoy my time on the river, and stopped worrying about complaints from the kids, all was well. I was in charge, sitting on the front of the canoe with the my husband Charlie at the back, navigating rocks below the shallow waters.

After about an hour of playing on the river, we had all mastered some simple skills. Eventually we got over to the muddy banks, where withies grew abundantly. Pulling the canoe across the mud and roping our vessel up to a tree, we found a seat in the form of a stump, and there ate our prepared cucumber sandwiches. Under the canopy of withies we looked about us to find that we had company, in the shape of many washed-up items from the high waters of winters before. A septic tank was half submerged in mud, along with a salt barrel and even a large plastic skip with wheels, perhaps from a supermarket.

Returning to the river, we travelled a little further upstream. The sun was hot and flickered on the water, making mirrors. Little fish swam in shoals about the shallows, while the river weed we call 'mermaids' hair' wavered thick and silky in the sunlight below the clear waters. There was a gentle summer flow upon the river, with the sounds of soothing trickles, as the river busied on by.

Turning our canoe back downstream, we curved about the banks of the river to enjoy a floating rest, and were blissfully carried down with its gentle flow. The children enjoyed getting close to the banks and the wildlife within. Proud swan parents guarded their fluffy grey cygnets, for it was here the babes were born, nests made all bunchy and comfy with scatters of downy chick feathers. Preening is the order of the day for all, and nothing much distracts their family grooming. Mother ducks hid in pockets in the river bank under drapes of withy, hurriedly rounding up their babes as we passed them by. The yellow balls of fluff with tiny little faces bobbed lightly on the waters surface like leaves.

A little further down the river, the canoeing experience began to wane somewhat and the canoe became difficult to handle. As it started to twirl, with screams from the children, we suddenly hit a rock in mid-river. It caught us in the middle, and there we were stuck unbalanced like a seesaw.

We were not able to get off this rock. The 'rudder system' on the canoe (Charlie) was not doing his bit. He was busy lying back with his feet up on each side of the gunwales, drinking a can of beer. 'It's Dad's fault!' they complained. 'He's falling asleep!' And who could blame him, with Nature's own tranquillity and added benefits?

This is one part of that first river trip that the children would not forget, and now they are grown up they still talk about it.

The following year, Charlie and I purchased a canoe of our own. It was a sixteen-foot Rolex Mad River in cherry red, weighing eighty pounds. She was a stable vessel, and sat well in the water.

We had many happy years on the Wye with our children and their little friends - it was very good of the mothers to trust us with their own children. I feel so proud to say that we shared and laid the foundations of many happy memories for our children and their friends as well.

CANOE MADNESS

Brave, crazy, over-confident or mad, take your pick, it's got to be at least two of the four. In October 2000 Charlie and I went forth on the River Wye. Not many people would have attempted this trip. I do not really recommend it unless you are experienced, and we were not. It hadn't been long since we had purchased a canoe of our own, and we had had only a few months' experience. The river has two faces - calm and polite, or fast and raging. A few surprises are expected along the way, as the river is always changing, but don't trust it, ever – respect it.

I have a name for our canoe; I call it "Standing Bear" after an American Indian of the 1800s. Strong and proud, stable and true, the name fits our canoe. She is tough enough to take knocks and crashes with her stable buoyancy. She sits well in the water, not so streamlined as to cut the surface, but safe. The drawback is that she's a pig of a weight to pull up the river banks and steps at Yat or Monmouth. Lifting her above the shoulders to put her up on to a truck roof rack is a real challenge.

The few small steps at Kerne Bridge, where everyone lowers their canoes into the water, were fully submerged today, and the river was not looking polite. But the challenge for us was irresistible, if darned scary. We could have turned away and driven back to Tewkesbury, but Charles and I needed the thrill. We did for a while dither about it as our instincts got in the way. A couple turned up behind us, having the same idea, with their canoe still fixed to their car. When they had seen the great swell of the river they told us that they were not going to risk it because it was moving too fast and rising.

Wise move, I thought, but still we defied the odds. They looked on in horror as we jumped into our canoe and sailed away with no effort to the paddles. As we gave a little tap here and a little tap there to the water, with paddles steering to keep straight, I felt as if we were alone on an ocean. The river was so wide, and baby did we motor on that surface, the flow was so fast.

Concentration was a must, as we had company alongside us on both sides of the canoe in the shape of most of the logs and tree trunks in Wales, along with a few complete trees. All this wood had been ripped from the banks and fields by the tide's grabbing flow. While paddling the river and wondering what might come our way.

I do remember in the closure of Thomas Woods that I caught sight of two men and their ladies taking a stroll along the footpath. They certainly did not expect to see people on the river today, and it said it all on their faces. They looked really shocked. Bloody fools, they must have thought.

Sometimes you would hear the glub of bubbling water underneath the canoe, and a whirlpool would appear where a massive log had got trapped under the water in a rock and was trying to get free against the river's great hauling pull. On one occasion, further down the river just by Lydbrook, a glub appeared in front of the canoe and my instinct told me we were in danger of capsizing if we did not steer away soon. So I called to Charles "Left turn now!" When we had passed on, we looked behind us to see that sure enough, a massive log was emerging, thrown up out from where it had been trapped under the water. Now bobbing and spinning on the river's surface, aiming in our direction, it flowed on towards us with the rest of the debris at speed.

Continuing down the raging torrent, there is only one way home, and that is to enjoy the ride (nutters!). Looking up from the banks to people walking along the field edges, we were high on top of the river surface, and now looking into the fields around. Mad mad mad, I thought, we might as well keep going and plough on to Symonds Yat, really I was so scared. There was no effort at all in this canoeing trip, as the river carried us on at such speed. We were shooting under bridges, such as the old railway bridge at Lydbrook, which I have always called Oil Drum Bridge because it looks black and dirty like a couple of big old oil drums. We were so high up on a flooded river that we were almost halfway up the legs of the bridge.

Further on down the river is the Huntsham Bridge,

where all the vacant birds' nests underneath can be seen close. These little birds that nest here in the summer have it right, being so close to the river. They skim the surface for flies in their millions, a constant food source for the babes in warmer calmer days.

Not much later on, approaching the hotel, there is a ferry pull wire across the river, so we had to duck low into the canoe to avoid getting decapitated. From the hotel, shocked looks from the residents standing on the balcony said it all, as we were the only mad hatters on the river that day. As we neared home we felt thankful to be dry, because the conditions were getting worse and we could have capsized so easily. It was a relief to reach the canoe launching centre.

As we neared the steep steps, a young man helped us to get our canoe off the river and on to our truck. When we told him about our mad adventure, he said no one should have been on the river today as it was fast rising, and they were not letting canoes out. In the fifteen minutes we had been talking almost a step had been covered by the waters. We looked out to see a dead sheep whizzing down, all blown up with its legs skyward. The poor thing could have come from anywhere, dragged out from a field; it had had no escape. The river will claim anything and anyone. Nevertheless it was adrenalin fuel to the max, and we gratefully lived to tell the tale.

Would we do it again? I am not really sure, but the memory is good, and you couldn't get any closer to a mad river than this.

This journey from Kerne Bridge to Symonds Yat launch canoe centre took us under one hour. I would like to stress that proper safety equipment was used, such as buoyancy jackets, helmets and throw ropes. It is best to take advice, and canoe only when it is safe.

STORMS & THORNS

〜

2001

We had not been canoeing the River Wye a year yet, but it was enough to gather the basics. Our visits to the river were a weekend respite from the hard working week now left behind us. I am forever surprised that we have the energy to do all this paddling, as our daytime jobs are as self-employed wall and floor tilers. Perhaps this line of work has given us the stamina to go canoeing, but I'm not too sure about our stamina after a day on the river.

My youngest daughter, Daisymay, who is nine, is still young enough to want to be with me, and today we will be going on to Monmouth. To cut the trip a little shorter than normal, we cast off at Huntsham Bridge. The river was full and it was a fair day, with moderate breezes.

We had been canoeing for an hour when we saw a mature couple in their canoe going our way downriver. We began a conversation, and they both appeared confident, and were clearly old hands at this game. Then it emerged that the gentleman was a canoeing instructor, and had been for many years. I remember feeling awkward, because I felt he might be watching our skills as we all paddled the Wye together. He did offer advice from time to time about the best way to use the paddles, which I valued.

We were fast approaching the rapids at Yat, and as we all passed under the ferry pull I told our new friends what we were all about to encounter, as they were not from this county. The rough ride ahead on the rapids is always scary, no matter how many times you have crossed this point. Although I want to master this monster, I still feel a little faint at its sight. Fear sets in when you start to wonder if you will end up a turbulent wet mess, chasing the canoe down the river after being thrown in, or the one who got away, still nice and dry, and very grateful, because somehow you got lucky and the rapids did not get you. I prefer not to think about it - just kill it and see.

Everything is fine on these rapids, so long as all hands are to the decks. You dig in with the paddles on both sides to balance the canoe, in turn mastering the tossing choppy waves, which come at you in all directions. There are big, dipping, gripping, black holes which eventually suck you in, then chuck you back out of the watery mouth, but only if you put up a fight. The thing to remember is, never hold on to the gunwales - all efforts are to the paddles. I learned that early.

As we were drawn into the rapids, I was determined to make an impression on our new-found professional friends, and not embarrass myself by falling in. While my daughter was petrified and began squealing like a piglet, the front end of the canoe (where I always sit) suddenly took a massive nose dive into the black hole, generously scooping up half the ruddy river and pouring it into the canoe. When the canoe came back up from its dive it chucked back into my face several gallons of freezing cold river water. I can tell you it knocked the wind out of my sails for sure. It was up my nose, in my eyes, I swallowed some of it (yuck), and got wet knickers to boot. The water then sloshed back up the canoe, past Daisy and up to Charlie.

Well we did it, and with an audience of kayakers watching our moves we headed further on downriver. One guy put his hand up in approval to us, while our accompanying friends managed the choppy waves, which roared turbulently and wildly over sunken boulders. The look of concentration on their faces as I looked back at them did not look much as if they were shelling peas. I think they too were hopeful of a dry escape.

We were now all bobbing on down to Biblins Bridge, and the waters became calmer. The silence and the trickling waters mirrored reflections of surrounding trees upon the river's surface. Soon enough the different sounds of approaching, shallow waters rushed over the pebbles and small rock, just under the swing bridge at Biblins. People were standing on the swing bridge, waving to us, and their children, never still, made the wires squeak as we shot underneath them.

Further on into deeper waters - the river here does have some depth to it - a commotion of animal noise arose upon the banks ahead. Slowing our canoes down, we all saw a mink chasing a small eel through the grassy banks down to the river. The mink was so engrossed that it did not notice us floating on the river, looking at it. What a racket it made as it ran to catch its slippery dinner. The little eel did put up a fight, trying to slither away through the grass at speed. When caught, the eel began curling and whipping its body around the mink's chops. But the mink got his dinner.

Paddling on towards Monmouth, just under the white limestone Sister Rocks above, all seemed fair and lovely on the river. An island of withy that has collected over the years has formed a small island in the middle of the river here, where swans nest and preen. River weed (mermaids' hair), grows abundantly here, blocking the route forward on the right. The left turn is best, around the island of withy. There is a rocky bottom with a good flow on the river this way. Low branches overhang into the river, but you can avoid them. At the same time the swans stretch out their necks in protest at your passing presence. "Too close!" they say with a hiss, "Goodbye!" we say, with a kiss.

Suddenly a wind started to blow hard, just around the corner from the withy island. Some say that the weather here can change without permission, but that's Wales anyway and we are nearly in Wales. The weather produces a tunnel effect, which makes it hard to steer straight in the side on gusts, which can easily turn our canoes in a spin.

It was damn hard work all the way to Monmouth and the winds did not let up. Our friends stayed with us, as I think they could see we might get thrown in. I did not want them to feel responsible for us, but they accompanied us all the same.

Almost reaching Monmouth, we all decided to pull into the shelter of banks to eat. We were all feeling tired, cold and weak from the hard canoeing, with the wailing winds head on in our faces. Poor Daisy was shivering from lack of activity, and we were concerned for her wellbeing. Monmouth could not come quick enough, but it was a long haul. As we all set off back to the river, it became too rough to paddle in the middle, so we kept close to the banks.

Then the distant sound of bleating came to us beyond the wind. This is all we need, I thought. A sheep was caught in the brambles which were growing at a slant on the river bank; the poor animal had got tangled in the thorny brambles while trying to get to longer grass. I'm sure this is how they often fall in and drown.

So there we all were hanging on in our canoes to the brambled banks, trying to free this sheep, which was making no effort to move, until our new woman friend bashed her paddle against the brambles, beat the bank and shouting "raah raah!" The sheep made a hasty retreat, jumping with fright and unhooking its curly coat from the brambles. If it had not been for the woman the animal would have been there all night, or maybe forever.

Eventually we all made it to Monmouth, freezing cold, wet through and exhausted. I felt bad for Daisy, and the weather was getting worse. The boys went to get the cars, and our lady friend waited with me, rubbing Daisy's cold white feet and talking to her as her own.

Strangers these people were, and we did not even ask their names - why I do not know. But their company was comforting. Conversation was not much exchanged along the river, but they stayed close, all the way.

When it was time to depart our dear friends' company, we never heard of or met them again. This was twelve years ago now, and I have wondered many times why things turn out as they do, and why we do not talk as we should. Perhaps our accompanying friends were angelics, looking after us? Whether they were earthly or heavenly beings, who knows what God is up to, when all seems too perfect.

BIRDS, BEES
& FAMILIES

∽

2001

In this year of 2001, my father Don died suddenly from an aneurysm. The shock and rawness of grief, and the disbelief, were hard to swallow, specially as he had seemed such a fit person. I always thought Dad would go on to be ninety-something like his dad, my grandad George, but then thoughts can be so deceiving, and life itself can be so fragile.

Dad was still working at seventy, and he did not really want to retire. He enjoyed his work and meeting all the people he knew through it. It was so important to him that he continued to give Tewkesbury's community his true services. He was so patriotic about his town, and really proud of Tewkesbury. Dad was a true Tewkesbarian (as we call ourselves) to the last.

When my great grandfather Bartholomew Sweet retired, he handed his company, B. Sweet & sons, Builders, Carpenters, and Undertakers, down to his son George, my grandfather. Then my grandfather, on his retirement, handed down the firm to my father. My dad did not get the chance to retire because he enjoyed his work so much, so when he passed away he handed his portion to his son, my brother Brett. The company is an old Tewkesbury family establishment, and funerals in the 1800s were horse-drawn affairs. There are pictures on the walls inside the office of the glass wheeled case that held the coffins. The glass carriage is flanked by two fine black horses, wearing feathered headbands upon their brows.

The old photograph on the office wall was taken outside Holy Trinity Church opposite, where a funeral was to take place opposite the firm's premises. In later years when cars were invented, my great grandfather's company was the first in Tewkesbury to own a car. More cars came along as times went on. When I was about ten, I still remember these old black hearses parked in my grandfather's Oldbury garages. They were very cumbersome and large, but they had the graceful and stylish design of the age.

★ ★ ★ ★ ★

Life for me and my little family, the family I had made with Charlie, had to manage without Dad, and thank goodness I could carry on. It was a strain most days to keep my chin up in the early months, because I missed my dad so much, as anyone would, but it did not stop me from feeling guilty for being happy, or laughing, or enjoying myself. I had to remind myself that these thoughts would grieve Dad if he knew I felt this way. He made me with Mum and gave me life so life, and happiness would be all he expected of me.

So... I learned to drive, and learned a second career in my husband's business, as a ceramic wall and floor tiler. Women did not turn up in these building trades much then, but I must admit I enjoyed the funny looks and the male attention. For many years I had a varied working life in the car industry before marrying Charlie, and then I stayed at home to bring three children up. Somehow I felt at times that my cup was nearly full, but it wasn't quite, thank goodness.

Family life was good, up to the point where a member of the family took advantage of my father's absence and split our families. This did not help the situation for my mother, as she was too weak to act after my father's death. It was as if things were not going on for the best, and they surely did not. The start of this damage involved my daughter being attacked by a dangerous new dog from an animal home, and the details are too painful to even write about. For my daughter, I can only say that she was maimed in mind, body and spirit, and the road to her recovery from this took two years. The cruelty that my own family experienced in this dark time by one person, cannot be written down.

★ ★ ★ ★ ★

Activities that had begun in the Forest for us, the camping

and canoeing on the Wye, every weekend, became a big part of my own family's life. Our friends and the children's friends took turns every other weekend, and all shared equally in our pastimes and joys.

Today it is a beautiful warm summer day, and the river is tranquil in every way as we drift downstream. Suddenly, without notice, our troubles have begun to swim away, like the little fish in the shadowed waters at the side when we ripple their sky as we pass by. Such beauties of nature within the river never cease to delight me; it is another world.

But the tranquillity is soon disturbed by a deep hum. The noise is somewhat familiar. I lift my eyes to the sky to see that the true blue of the sky has become dotted with black. There are squeals of concern from us all - I have never seen anything like this before. Just above us flies a vast swarm of bees. Never have I seen so many bees, all those beating wings. The sound is very loud; there must be thousands. I am scared for the children, and would think nothing of turning the canoe over and hiding under it submerged, in case they attack us. This might not have been likely, as I do not know much about bees. They may have been disturbed from a nest, or perhaps they were off to find a new one. Seconds passed, and so did these little creatures, until the great shadow had lifted back from the sky.

Passing peacefully through and under Kerne Bridge, voices and commotion are heard echoing through the woods. Past Thomas Wood, gunshots echo across the valley, and I wonder what has happened to the peaceful paddling. The girls, Daisymay and her friend Kayleigh, have put their little brollies up - and what luck they have, because suddenly and unexpected there comes a "thwack" - something nasty has hit one of the trees closest to us by the river. We all duck our heads low as a shower of lead shotgun pellets pepper all over us. Some of the pellets hit the canoe, then plop down into the river. Whatever is going to happen next?

Carrying on our journey downriver, we are now approaching the rocky beach and buttercup fields of Coldwell Rocks. We steer into the banks to stop off for lunch. The girls have their fishing nets to do their bit, trying to save and scoop up little fish that have got caught up in the pools left behind. When the swollen river came through last, fish got left behind as the river receded quickly back to normal. The pools of river water soon dry up and become too warm, lacking oxygen in the summer months, so the girls like to save the fish and put them back slowly into the cooler waters. When the fish are released from the girls' nets, after getting used to the colder waters of the river, they swim off gratefully into the flow. Some shelter underneath the mermaids' hair, which has attached its roots to the bottom of the rocky riverbed and flows long and silky green in the flickering sunlight.

Most of the river banks have collapsed at the edge, falling back down into the river's flow, and the fields are getting smaller because of it. The soils are then scooped up by the rising waters of the wet seasons when they come, washing what has fallen away downstream. Washed-up rock from the river bed then comes through and stops at these points, filling in the gaps of vacant field and producing little rocky 'beaches'. Then as nature takes over, lush green grasses seed themselves into the stones and rock, making a natural garden that we could not compete with. Nature is also good at claiming land, and wherever water lies or flows through, the landscape will forever be changing. I have watched the mighty Wye these few years getting wider in parts, because of higher waters. The weak riverbanks cannot take the pressure, and are easily scooped away.

The girls have played in the yellow fields behind us, and have been fed sandwiches and orange squash. We always had a tradition that before we all left, a creation of pebbles had to be stacked on the rocky beach. Each pebble is of different sizes, and shapes, interlocking into an artistic form. Funny how people appreciate our creations, for when we drop by this way every other weekend the pebbles are still there, where we left them last. We have done this at other locations along the river, and it soon caught on, because we started to notice that people were copying this craze of ours, which gave us a laugh when passing by. Then it seemed to become a kind of human message thing - "I like yours, do you like mine?" "I have seen yours, this is mine"... "Mine is higher than yours" etc.. It beats smoke signals for sure.

As we all get into the canoe and admire our pebbled

creations from the river, a mother and her little girl with a puppy come from the nearby fields to sit on the rocky beach by the river and rest. All is well until we hear an awful noise of shouting, and the closer barks and snarls of dogs, very large dogs, two of them; they come quickly into view, running mad from the fields, bounding towards us with what I perceive as aggression. Their large black and tan bodies, docked tails, and large heads, indicate a Rottweiler crossbreed, and I am on red alert.

The mother looks petrified and keeps still, protecting her child and puppy in a frozen embrace. Charlie tries to stop Daisy from screaming, as a dog attack she experienced not long before is still real for her. My thoughts in seconds are to jump in the canoe, get this mum and her child and puppy into the river and into my canoe, but while this catastrophe is unfolding a foreign man appears from the fields trying to look angry. He whips the dogs' leads in fury and shouts to them in what sounds like Italian. As he comes down the bank, he slashes one of the cowering dogs with its lead. It makes a bellowing sound as he beats its body, and the other dog legs it back up the bank, knowing its fate if it stays around.

I lost the plot at that point, and shouted over to the man "You bloody idiot, get your dogs under control! Get out of here, and stop being so damn cruel!" He looked straight at me then in utter shame, which satisfied my anger to a point. So with steely looks from me, to show I was ready for action, and with my hands on my hips as I stood upright in my canoe, he gathered his dog, took to his heels and disappeared into the green.

Daisy was sobbing, and her pal Kayleigh tried to soothe her. Charlie looked gaunt, and I was seething. Mom, child and puppy looked grateful for the support. We turned to paddle away from them downriver and I bid them farewell. As we paddled on I wondered what would happen next.

The trip back to Symonds Yat was fairly good. The girls soon perked up. Kayleigh came into our lives at the right time, and fitted in with our family. She lived in the next street to us; her family had come down from Somerset. Kayleigh came everywhere with us, even on holidays to the coast, where we all stayed with our parents in their big house in Lyme Regis. I love Kay as my own, and she is as close as my own daughter.

When we had all shored up and got back to my waiting car at Yat, we began to heave the canoe up those deep, steep steps, with legs that were damp and cramped and tired. Once at the top, we tipped up the canoe to let all the water out, as little pools of water do collect in the bottoms of canoes when you have children on board. All packed up and ready to go, the canoe was soon on the roof of my Freelander, tied safe and secure.

We set off to drive to Charlie's waiting car at the other end, but as I turned the wheel to set off, the front end of the canoe mysteriously bent further over my bonnet, like a big old banana. A crack? Oh no! Charlie and I looked at each other. One of us, as we argued it out stupidly, had not tied the front rope up at the front of the canoe, and I had run over the dangling rope with my front wheel, pulling the canoe against the car. We did not want to look, because the crack sounded like big damage.

Upon getting out and unleashing the trapped rope, we saw that the wooden gunwale had split and the blue coating to the canoe had cracked deep. The damage underneath we did not know. At this point I felt like running and jumping back into the river unaided.

This canoe cost us £2,000 from North Wales and was made of Kevlar, so I thought it should be tough. Later on in the week, it turned out that all was well, with only minor repairs needed; the main body of the canoe was not damaged. Now there I was minding my own business, trying to be positive, not daring to even think, "I wonder what is going to happen next". In the Forest or on the River Wye, you never know what is going to happen next. So just keep smiling and remember, you will always have a story to tell 'em when you get old.

HOARWITHY MOON

LATE SUMMER 2003

It is hard to believe that my younger daughter Daisymay was 10 years old when we first came to Hoarwithy. As I write this in May 2010, it is a few days since she turned 17. Our children have all grown up now and flown the nest, but the fact remains that we camped and canoed with them for many years, giving them and their little friends many happy and water-filled memories for the rest of their lives.

I remember when we came down the river last year, Hoarwithy was a little gem of a find. Today we are driving the small road to Hoarwithy, which is canopied with the draping withies along the banks of the Wye. The little road soon comes to a place called Hole in the Wall, and our blue and red canoes sit on top of our trucks as we wind our way down through this narrow dusty country lane alongside fields where barley and wheat grow. Farmers' dogs dart out from their yards and run freely from farm to farm down the lane. There is not a lot of room down these lanes, and you just hope no one is coming up the opposite way. At worst a field tractor might steam through here at any moment, taking the whole lane up.

We soon arrive in the sleepy village of Hoarwithy, where time seems to have stopped still. On the road through, over the river bridge, horses walk by regularly, almost as if cars did not exist. It is possible to imagine being transported back to times of old, when life was so simple. It is so quiet here, and all that can be heard is the quiet voices of people and the animals in the neighbouring fields.

There's a little pub through this way by the name of the New Harp Inn. A year ago the inn was still an old-style concern, with basic food, good beer and a pool table, all that is expected of a country inn. The old photographs on the walls told stories past of the river's visits through this establishment. But where I come from living by rivers, you go with the flow (ha ha), clean up and carry on with business.

The old post office here at Hoarwithy is not used any more and is now vacant. The windows are full of rubbish, papers and old leaflets. The Italic church over the way, which is the main feature in this landscape, is still very active. The beautiful architecture was I'm told crafted by Italians who came to this country to work on this church, making it what it is today, a real gem within its landscape and in need of worshippers.

Alongside the New Harp there is a gated entrance to fields with sheep and cattle grazing peacefully. The bottom fields are cordoned off by a fence and gates to separate the camping area from the livestock. Canoes are constantly being launched here on to the Wye. These fields and land are owned by Mrs Roberts of Tresseck Farm. The first time we met her was early on a cold dewy morning, when she rudely shook the tops of everyone's tents with a firm hand, saying in a strict voice "Come on, time to pay up!" She was certainly on the ball, and kept everything in good working order. Her voice rang out through the early morning air as she called to us to "Make sure you bag up all your rubbish and put it in the bins provided, and no fires unless given permission!" She could have been a town crier, she really scared me.

In later years we found that Mrs Roberts was the sister of a milk farmer up the Ashchurch road near where we live in Tewkesbury. This is where we buy our Christmas tree every year. It certainly is a small world I thought, and examining the family resemblance I would say that Mrs Roberts and her brother look very alike.

I remember one Christmas when the children were younger and we went to buy a tree for Christmas, he showed the children around his milk parlour. The cows looked gigantic, as they were being milked at a higher level. The milk freshly drawn from the cows swirled around in a big vat. I remember how the sweet smell of the warm milk from the cows gave a comforting aroma.

Getting back to Hoarwithy, there were choice places around the site for open fires for the night, and it was a race to get one. In the daytime we gathered wood from the forest to cook on and keep warm. This kept us going all night, and the fire was still alight in the morning as orange embers. At night, as the fire got going, we would cook sausages, burgers and baked potatoes, and in the morning, if you fancied putting some more burgers on the fire for breakfast, it was still hot enough to do it, if you could still stomach the thought after a skinful of beer the night before. Whenever you left your allotted camping place to canoe or walk the surrounding fields of Hoarwithy, it really was held in trust for other campers to respect your fire, and the wood you had collected for the coming night. But we never had trouble, just a lot of laughter.

On this weekend in 2003 it was very humid, so the next day we decided to have a cool day playing in and on the river. We owned many buoyancy jackets and gave them to every child with us - Daniel, Daisymay, Kayleigh, Kiren, Shannon and Katie, as well as two other adults, our dear friends Mike and Sandra who were with us. So the responsibility for all the children was shared. We spent the day mucking about on the river paddling in circles, as it was very low and there was hardly any flow except in the deeper parts up river.

As I sat between two Land Rovers by the tents, trying to keep cool from the burning sun, I was sketching with charcoal the backdrop of pine trees in the distance on the hillside. The children were laughing and playing on the river to their hearts' content. As I peeked over the hedges to the river down below, all I could see was a line of happy children, arm in arm walking up the river, all with their buoyancy jackets on. The river really was that low, and came just above their ankles in some parts. I will cherish this memory of them all forever and with such joy, as it is what childhood is all about. This, I thought, is happiness remembered in our hearts and minds forever.

The day wore on, and the sun burned orange as it sank into the blue cloudless sky. There were many hungry mouths to feed, so it was soon time to light our fire and cook the kiddies' favourites on the camp fires. The children were free to play in the fields all night, though eventually it was too dark to see anything away from the fire.

We adults enjoyed many beers while sitting in our deck chairs laughing, reminiscing and warming our toes against the flames. Our faces were red from sun and beer, and with the whiffs of smoke from the fire it was a camping delight.

Suddenly from out of the pitch black, star-spangled sky a bright light appeared, rising up from the other side of the river behind the hill – the full moon. It rose steady and full and strangely larger that I had ever seen it. As it emerged, with every second the night sky came alive, casting a great light up on to the pitch black fields and beyond. Its size was incredible. I have never in my life seen the moon that big. The earth must have been very close to the moon at this time, and I will never forget it. The river was lit up with twinkles of light upon its waters as the water gently flowed on by.

As the night went on the children snuggled into their

sleeping bags by the fire, their full bellies and tired eyes quickly sending them to sleep under the stars. Animal noises of the night were many, as we stayed up by the fire and listened to owls and all manner of night-time foragers close by and further off into the night. There must have been foxes not far from us, as dogs barked repeatedly and then we heard the scuttling of clacking hens running about a pen. The dogs were in the house and the cunning fox played his merry tune of mischief. I was expecting gunshots. None came out of the dark, but I hoped the fox had not got his way tonight. I thought of those poor biddy chickens, as I call them, and wondered why the blasted fox has to kill them all.

It was time to retire, and the children needed shifting back into their tents, so we lifted them up by the ends of their sleeping bags and pulled them along the grass, then lifted them into the tents with great difficulty. Not one of them woke. As the fire dimmed to orange embers, we gave a last look up into the starry night, stretching on and on forever into the universe. The moon sat high, looking smaller now but still sending its luminous white light across the landscape. The river twinkled as its soft ripples were caught by our Hoarwithy moon. That day and a night became like magic in our hearts and minds forever, in that beautiful place called Hoarwithy.

MESSING ABOUT
ON THE RIVER

~

As we launched our canoe at Kerne, the early morning was fresh and new and the sun came up slowly with the coming day of August. Sweet scents of grassy fields and flowers filled the air, and damp earthy mists from the river danced across its surface. Soft white veils of river mist drifted upriver like a ghost, then the mist dispersed as it went on, away up to the sky.

It is great to be out on the river so early this morning. A while back we took a trip to North Wales and bought a canoe of brightest blue. It is made of tough Kevlar, has wooden gunwales and weighs 60lbs, which is much lighter than our previous canoe (which we still have.) Our new canoe was instantly named by me Crazy Horse after an American Indian of the 19th century. I have this thing that all transport has to have an individual name. Our new canoe feels very different. Crazy Horse sits really well in the water, and its performance is fast and smooth as it cuts the water with determination.

As we push away from the lush green banks, mud is stirred from our movements; the river is low today. The long hot days of summer reveal minnows in shoals, picking about the silts in the shallows. To the middle part of the river, a lamprey swims close by our canoe and we watch her as she swims gracefully along by the side of us, keeping silent to watch the lamprey as she snakes the river bed at speed within the low clear waters below, caring not what is above.

Further upriver, the silence is broken by a silver scaly salmon who makes his entrance out of the water behind us and crashes with an almighty splash back down into the river. I just glimpsed his tail disappear back down into the river - he (or she) was a whopper. I have heard stories of fish jumping out of rivers and into boats. Charlie jokes to me that if this salmon had jumped into our canoe by mistake, we would have bashed him and kept him for tea. But I am not hungry enough to do such a thing. Perhaps that is why I have too much concern for creatures great and small. I am sure we would have put Mr Salmon back in his home. But if he had knocked himself out, job done, he would indeed have been tea.

As we paddle on the air becomes humid but fresh with morning. Our paddles rest on the gunwales, as drips of water fall back to the river off them, making bangled rings upon its surface. The rings widen towards the banks within this still millpond flow.

We are all alone now, messing about on the river. As the morning sun becomes stronger in warmth and light, we drift on and on, feeling more of the movements below and around us. We share Mars Bars between us and Charlie has a nibble of one, then slides it back up the canoe to me. The morning's silence is broken as we pass a distant wooded enclosure, just over the river bank, and into the fields beyond. Echoing disagreements of flapping crows are breaking out in the tops of the tall pine trees overhead. In times of higher waters, when we passed this way we would see an old wooden canoe which had been dragged up into the woods and tied to a trunk; it never seemed to move.

On our left, by the side of the river, is a lush and wild flower covered piece of land with many species of trees. Within this bounty fair of wild flowers and grasses stands our old friend the oak, my landmark, by Bishopswood. Upon passing him, I view once again his seasonal state, which is ever changing. Our old timer is veteran in years, but still looking good.

Further on downriver, in the shades of an overhang of trees, an elderly man stands at the end of his garden, which backs out on to the river. He looks surprised to see someone out so early on the waters, and gives us a word from across the waters that we can't quite hear. Not wanting to paddle on and be rude, we think he might want company, so we paddle over to him, to have a morning chat.

We have talked for some time now, and the morning coolness has waned. The sun is getting hot, and I am sweating. This chap can talk for England, and he does so as

I hold on to thick roots growing out of the river bank. The canoe keeps drifting out, so I occasionally pull it back in, drawing on a thick root. We have soon been talking for a good while. He says his name is Jack Garrett and he has lived there since 1970. Jack was a lovely man, and very sweet. He told us about his childhood and his father, and a fishing trip with Prince Charles.

Behind him as Jack talked I could see the figure of a little old lady in a pinny, who stood silently listening, back in the darkness of the garden. I think she was his wife, and she was probably wondering where Jack had got to, because we had been talking for ages.

Jack did make me laugh when he complained at all the toilet paper and poop he had had to remove down the years from his river frontage. Passing canoeists would use it, but there were more laughs in that conversation about knickers, which I will not relate. But on a nicer note, he said that in the very early morning, looking out on to the river from his garden, you could often see the deer coming out of the woods to drink water from the river. It sounded like my kind of place.

Soon afterwards we bid him farewell, and he looked happy as we went on our way downriver again. Although we lost time, it was lovely to make someone's day, because it certainly made ours and created yet another memory.

NETTLE TEA &
SKINNY-DIPPING

∽

SUMMER 2004

It was a hot day for canoeing, and even the early morning had no chill. Our day was to start at Ross, and it was going to be a long one. The landlord at the Hope & Anchor said we could park at his pub if we spent some money there, so we said that when we returned from the river at the end of the day, we would have a meal. We were ones for keeping our word, as the launching here at Ross is easy. The steps that lead down to the river are not too steep. It is a pleasant trip away from here, paddling the curve to face Wilton Bridge, choosing which bridge arch to go through.

Once under the bridge, the approaching island of withies in the middle of the river opposite the White Lion public house has at this time of year a small number of nesting Canada geese. House martins also have nested for decades, maybe more, at the White Lion. With the river so close by, it is the perfect food source for the babes waiting under the eaves and roof spaces. The parents' skilled flight techniques are a wonder to watch, as their squeals echo through the sky and they dip and dive like little Spitfires, constantly on the wing just above the river's surface, scooping up the plentiful insect population.

Further on down the river, a heron in awkward flight is desperate to find rest as it circles the tree tops trying to get away from a black mob of scratchy crows, which are making a right din. They are sharp at the heels of the heron, who got too close to the crows' treetop nests. He falls lanky and grey back down to the river's safe haven. Further on downriver, up past and over the banks where crops are growing in the fields beyond, generator motors loudly chug away. The generators have pipes attached to them, leading down to the river, sucking gallons of water up to feed the crops.

Soon enough, we approach Coldwell Rocks, which peak out grey amid the rich green trees which have commandeered every nook and cranny of the rock face. From the heights peregrine cries echo down the valley, their babes in the rocks above the river. The river now becomes quite low, and in some places along the banks the flow is still and stagnant. Mosquito-infested pools swirl murkily, and it is good to get back out into the middle of the river afresh, into a clearer and gentle summer flow.

Just around the corner there is a small piece of flat bank which the river has moulded over the years into what we call the Beach. Grey rocks have fallen in and have been moved about, rolled and crumbled, by the river's flow. Crockery from neighbouring cottages has caught and settled here along the rocky beach over the years, and we collect more every time we stop here. Some of the artwork on the china is still colourful and elegant. One day I will make a collage picture from these old forest crocks.

It is here that we moor up to have lunch. The flow of the river pulls you in, but it will pull you back out again, if you do not steer, as the flow of water is fast. It is hard not to scrape the bottom of the canoe when we stop, and Charlie often moans about all the scratches on it. It is far from new and blue now, I say to him, joking that perhaps it is his weight pressing the canoe down. Then he says, "You're the one who's on the front, wench". Cheek!

The afternoon has become hot and humid, and the horseflies are a dammed nuisance. Today they are biting man and beast equally well. As we sit down to relax, the trickling waters glimmer and glint stars of sunlight back to the eye. The soft sounds of water are a delight, enough to send a baby to sleep. Time to eat, not to sleep. We delve into our dry bag for food.

But we soon discovered that in the dry bag, there was not a teabag, or any milk, in sight, just a flask of hot water. My throat was like the bottom of a dried-up well, and I was dying for a brew. Well that was that, I threw my toys out of the canoe, and complained like a teaoholic. The next thing I knew, Charlie had disappeared into the fields beyond, and as I sulked, he came back to me with nettles from the fields.

He poured hot water on to them, which I thought was so sweet of him, and gave me nettle tea. The nettles tasted so refreshing, and the tea was gladly and gratefully received, with a little tinge of guilt.

Charlie was wearing his shorts, and he soon became irritated and began to do a jungle dance, swatting at the horseflies like mad. He thought they had followed him out of the fields. I noticed after a time that an insect had settled on his leg. I pointed out that it was a horsefly. He gave a yelp, and smacked it. There was blood splattered on his leg, indicating that the damn thing had been having a good suck. So I joked to him that he should not be such a tasty geezer.

After lunch, we both decided that it would be nice to go for a skinny dip in the river, if only to get rid of the flies. The next thing I knew I had been seduced into stripping down to my panties. As I gave myself wantonly to the river's waters, it felt so good to feel the force of its flow against my body. I disappeared slowly up to my neck and floated on my back, holding on for anchor to the mermaids' hair, silky and wavering in the sunlight, flowing all one way on the river bed underneath me. I had now gone past caring if anyone could see me, even those above with binoculars on the rock, now viewing more than feathered birds today. While Charlie's eyeballs were popping out on strings, my perkies were raised buoyant to the sky.

I did with you feel as one,
this ancient rock crevice bend,
that the River Wye has forth come,
born from mountains, to the oceans,
forever, there will be no end.

It was not long before the silence was broken by fellow canoeists approaching our way. I do not know if they were going to stop off here or were just passing through. There were three canoes. One man looked at me as I dived for cover and smiled at me like the Cheshire Cat, but the woman accompanying him gave me a sharp look, then paddled off into the future with her nose in the air.

Well, this skinny-dipping had to stop some time, so we climbed out and got dried in our big fluffy towels, packed up and paddled away from the land of tranquillity. A mile up the river, we found these canoeists dining in a clutch of withy along the riverbank. Perhaps they had wanted to stop for lunch on the beach after all. As I passed them, all shy and girly, the gentleman in question shouted over "You can come and have a bathe in here if you like!" I'm not one for causing trouble, and quickly paddled away into my own future - this book.

IDLE DAYS OF
SUMMER

◞

JULY 2004

An early morning with clear skies looked promising for a good long day's canoeing. We decided to travel to Hereford and go downriver to Hoarwithy. We knew an early start was important, as this trip would take the best part of a day. We would take the tent and some small camping bits in case the trip became too much. Then if we needed to, we could stop overnight along the way. We had no intention of stopping overnight really, because we wanted to see if we could do this trip in one day.

Battling through the traffic at Hereford, we eventually found the canoe launching site. Both our trucks had to be taken, so one truck could be left at the start and the other at the launching site, giving us transport at each end of the trip.

As we launched our canoe at Hereford, the day was already getting hot. Parts of the banks were dried up and looking dusty from lack of rain, and there was very little flow. As we passed out through the town, a park close by the river frontage was full of people enjoying the summer heat, reading books and having picnics while children played. The banks along the way were standing firm with old thick willows which bowed their long wisps into the water's edge, gracefully stroking the warm, still river.

Once out of Hereford's bustle, the river downstream remained wide. We did take a bite of lunch on the way down, while we were in motion on the river in the canoe. Charlie used the end of his paddle like a tray, passing a cup of tea down to me at the front. Sandwiches came too, in the same fashion. I must say, it does not get better than this.

The flow got deeper and stronger as we paddled on. We caught up nicely on time into the day, as we still had a long journey home. Not that we were trying to rush on, as we were hoping to see something different along these waters, not having been this far up the river before.

The sun was now beaming upon us quite hot, but the coolness of the waters, with earthy river breezes that gently kissed my face and caressed my hair, was lovely. Wildlife was abundant within the banks of withies. Wildfowl and moorhens, all with their fluffy babes, preened and cleaned the day away. A pair of swans showed off their six downy grey cygnets, the parents watching with steely eyes over their young. From afar, a willowy grey heron stood on one leg, resting in the withies upon a dry river bank. Herons won't let you get too close to them, and that's the way it has always been, no matter how still you keep, as you drift on by. They are quite shy birds, so it's not long before they fly off to more private reaches of the river.

As we drifted on, my eye caught a glint of blue – a kingfisher. He did not notice us as we drifted into the closeness of the banks. He perched proud on a thin branch, with a small fish in his mouth. These tiny birds' colours flicker electric blue as the sunlight catches them in flight, skimming low and fast across the waters. What joys these are to reap in summertime.

Further down this tranquil way, in the distance we spied a large boat which was slightly on its side. It was strange to see this barge resting upon the flat silty banks. As we approached, I took photographs. This was a good excuse to get out and stretch the old river legs. We pulled our canoe on to the dried-out mudbank, all cracked from the summer heat, and the canoe looked like a toy compared to the barge. The name on the side was *Wye Invader*. Chained and secured, she was well-kept and tidy, but what was she doing there?

I think she must have been a working barge at one time, because there were pulleys and levers and wheels. Vacant she looked, no one was inside, but the sight of her reminded me of the old bible story of Noah. Tilted on her side, she looked as if she was patiently waiting for the waters to rise.

A few months later, I painted this barge from my photograph. Then a few years later there was a piece in the *Hereford Times* about her, with a picture of the owner, a gentleman called Mr Frank Barton. This answered my questions of a few years earlier. I have kept this newspaper cutting, and always hoped to contact Mr Barton one day because I have a picture of his barge for him.

The day's canoeing from Hereford to Hoarwithy was done in a day; it was getting on into the evening when we arrived, but we did it. The haul was long, but the river was kind to us. However our skin was feeling a little tight from the sun's rays, and our muscles from the paddling.

We did reward ourselves later in the evening with a crisp, cool beer at the White Lion at Ross. Bailey the resident labrador wanted to play as we supped our beer on the river bank. With never-ending energy, he kept going into the water and returning to shake himself all over us, because we wouldn't go down to the river to play ball. I think we have had enough water today, thank you Bailey.

MEMORIAL TO A DROWNED BOY

SEPTEMBER 2004

At the foot of Coldwell Wood by the River Wye is a monument. Its stonework and iron railings are very skilfully and beautifully made. It faces the river from higher ground, as at this very place, a young man lost his life in front of his parents and siblings. It was a sorrowful day indeed, in the lives of this dear family.

This is the inscription:

Sacred to the memory of John Whitehead Warre. who perished near this spot while bathing in the River Wye in sight of his parents, brother and sisters on 14th September 1804

In the 16th year of his Age

GOD'S WILL BE DONE!

Who in his mercy hath granted consolation to the parents of the dear departed in the reflection that he possessed.

Truth, innocence, filial piety and fraternal affection in the highest degree. That but a few moments before he was called to a better life he had. (with a never to be forgotten piety) joined his family in joyful thanks to his maker for the restoration of his mother's health. His parents in justice to his amiable virtues and excellent disposition declare he was void of offence towards them. With humbled Hearts they bow to the Almighty's dispensation, trusting thro the meditation of his blessed so He will mercifully receive their child He so suddenly took to himself!

This Monument is here erected to warn parents and others to be carefull how they trust the deceitfull stream and particularly to exhort them to learn and observe the directions of the Humane Society for the recovery of persons apparently drowned Alas! it is with the extremest sorrow here commemorated what anguish is felt from the want of this knowledge.

The lamented youth swam very well, was endowed with great bodily strength and activity and possibly, had proper applications been used. might have been saved from his untimely fate. He was born at Oporto in the kingdom of Portugal on the 14th of feb 1789. Third son of James WARRE of London and of the county of somerset Merchant and ELEANOR . Daughter of THOMAS GREG of Belfast Esq .

PASSENGER. who ere thou art spare this Tomb. It is erected for the benefit of the surviving being but a poor record of the grief of those that witnessed occasion of it -

God preserve you and yours from such calamity - And not
require their assistance. but you unfortunately should. With
directions for their application by the Humane Society for
the savings of persons apparently drowned are lodged at the
church of Coldwell

COAPE & SEALY LONDON 1805

The decay of this monument's stonework is apparent, and
the acid rain of our times has not helped. Words are missing
due to the crumbling of the stone face. Decorative carvings
are falling away with time, and it is a sure shame that this
monument is not preserved, as it serves a great purpose of
warning to everyone down the centuries.

FIELDS OF YELLOW

EARLY SUMMER 2004

This year the fields along the River Wye are abundant and
beautifully yellow with buttercups. Just under Coldwell
Rocks, and from the river over to the fields, I have never
seen these fields so rich in buttercups as they are this year.
My children and the children of friends we brought with us
on our canoeing trips here are now long grown up, but I will
forever hear their little voices of laughter across these fields
as they run free through the long lush grasses and
multitudes of buttercups and clover like spring lambs,
disappearing until we see only the tops of their hair bobbing
about the grasses. They hide from each other with their
games and then busy themselves among the buttercups and
clover and talk in their soft voices to each other while
making their buttercup bracelets and necklaces.

The softly-flowing river flickers on with the dancing
mirrors of summer sunshine upon its surface, and the silky
threads of mermaids' hair sway gracefully to and fro with the
shallow downstream flow. And upon the great mat of bobbing
river daisies which bloom from the mermaids' hair, there are

thousands upon thousands of white flowers with yellow centres – water crowfoot. These river daisies wilfully open up their little cups to the warm rays of summer warmth.

It was on this part of the river below Coldwell Rocks that I once saw a lamprey in the side shallows of the river, carrying a pebble in her sucker mouth. She was placing these collected pebbles, so neat and motherly, gently on to her nest under the water. So busy was she, that little lamprey, that she did not notice me looking at her maternal activities from my canoe on the surface above her. I wrote a poem, which became locked in my mind, and it goes like this.

These fields of yellow where children play
The flowing river lies low beside
Armfuls of buttercups reflect their youth
Sunlight and laughter bury their joys
Coldwell rocks above where babies cry
And skies of blue where mummy flies.

Fields of yellow as fondness unfolds
Where little children nestle to disappear
Among clover pink and buttercup chains,
My memories to you will now be told
Growing fondly vivid, in one mind's eye,
Remembering now a mother's small tear.

Forget you not as we grow old,
Forever on those fields of yellow,
Timeless ours, you are our gold.

KING OF THE RIVER

SUMMER 2004

There have been times of plenty, and then more than plenty, and then a little less, and then not enough – water, that is, in the river Wye. And today, at the height of summer, it is not quite enough. The river looks as if it is gasping, so gentle is the flow. Salmon stay close to the middle of the river, and that is where we paddle as we follow the salmon's slow way downriver, where the depths are greater. In some places the banks create stagnant whirls as the low waters reveal shoals of minnows picking away at the silt in the flickering sunlight.

The swans along the banks are more hissy than usual and are looking less content, thanks to the constant presence of the canoeists. Their grey cygnets, in broods of four to six, keep close by their parents along the riverbanks, seeming to carry the facial expressions of human children as if they are wondering "what's that?"

Both young and adult swans busy themselves with the cleaning of their fluff and feathers, preening the sunny days away. The beds of straw that had once formed their nest, so carefully woven and placed by their beaks, has no interest for mother now, as she has her brood to look after and is ready to teach the kids a bit of weed fishing.

The approach on the river, in the cool silent enclosure of Coldwell Rocks, gives us a sudden fearful view of a remarkable male swan, one I have found for a few years now in the same location. Once again it is that time of year when this bird will be at his worst, and every traveller on the river has to take his turn to face the wrath of this feisty swan. Just ahead of us you are guaranteed to hear the squeals and screams and harsh deep voices of men shouting at them to "gerroff!". Then there will be a splash and the bashing of paddles against the water as folk scramble to get past the swan's territory. We begin to take our turn reluctantly, knowing our fate, and prepare for the worst.

Canoes and kayaks sit pretty close to the water, so you are at a similar level to the wildlife, and this is not a good thing today. Oh no! Here he comes, his neck tucked in tight, his massive white angelic wings arched for maximum attack. The waters divide, fountaining each side of him, rushing past his puffed-up breast as he cuts the waters with determination. Soon he is lungeing towards us with his strong white neck, almost coming into the canoe, and hissing like a cobra. You can't help but squeal, for he is really scary, so you have to paddle fast, and paddle we do. Hell for leather we go.

This swan has never been seen on the river since 2004. I

wondered why, and began to have the awful thought that someone may have been cruel enough to kill him because they were fed up with his temper. Poor creature! I do hope this was not the case, as I would have been glad to put up with him. He did create a challenge, but he was only protecting his home and family. I do so miss this swan, as he became a legend of the river and a great talking point for many.

The swan had not moved up or down the river or anywhere else, because I have never encountered a swan like him since. Canoeing down the years since, from Hereford through to Monmouth, not one swan on the river has ever been like him. Then one afternoon in 2012 I was reading an issue from the previous year of my brother-in-law Len's vintage motorcycle club magazine and spotted in the obituaries a gentleman by the name of Tony Windeatt. It said that Tony used to delight in telling stories, including one about how he canoed the river Wye and was attacked by a swan. I was shocked to read this, as I had had the same experience. I wonder how many people from all over the country, down the years, who have canoed this stretch of river still remember this famous swan.

HARVEST, HOPE
& HOUNDS

LATE SUMMER 2004

There was a time when camping at Hoarwithy for the weekend with the children and their little friends was the best place in the world to be, within a place that time had forgotten. Hoarwithy is a place of bountiful seasons, where in the autumn we often come to pick elderflower and elderberry for my homemade wine. I have done this for years, and it is quite true that flower and berry wines really do taste different according to the places and soils they have grown from. Hoarwithy's creamy, lacy blooms of elderflower, growing in fields close to the river, are indeed a peasant's champagne.

My wine made can be light and fragrant in taste, with the aroma of muscat if fewer flowers are used, but in the past I have been over-generous, using too many flowers and making my wine taste stronger, with the aromas of tomcat. After making this mistake, my trick was to use lemonade to disguise the strong scents of tomcat, making an elderflower spritzer instead when entertaining.

Hoarwithy's elderberries, when the season arrives, have a deep colour. They are always fat and juicy and produce a dark and porty wine. The wines have a distinctive earthy taste to them, which is the original Hoarwithy aroma of this fair land. Her rich foliages derive from an earthy soil which is constant in rich nutrients, from the rising river and the livestock that graze here. Fresh abundance comes out of all that grows in the bosom of Hoarwithy.

Blackberries are plentiful when their season has come, growing fat and juicy within the hawthorn bushes that divide the fields of livestock. Hops will climb and grow sparse here, and hang gracefully from the tree branches into and along the tops of the hawthorn bushes. We take the hops home for decoration, as there is not enough to make beer with - sorry Charlie. Here in the dampness of the dewy fields grows food fit for a king.

Hoarwithy mushrooms develop to the size of dinner plates and grow abundantly in these fields close by the river, but when their time comes you have to harvest them early, as the worms soon weave their way into the tops and spoil them.

★　★　★　★　★

It is Saturday today and the month of June is upon us. We will be getting on the river soon, as we manoeuvre the canoe down the now dried-out muddy banks. The steps here have nearly all disappeared with the rising waters of winters past, so we rope up and let the canoe slide down to the river. Kayleigh and Daisy are equipped with new water pistols which we bought them at Ross, and I think to myself, what trouble have we got ourselves into now, as they sit giggling with each other, in the middle of the canoe? They certainly won't be short of water, that's for sure, the little minxes.

The girls are now ready and eager to set sail, their little bodies shiny with spray lotion to protect their delicate skins from the sun. As we begin to set sail upon the waters of the tranquil river, the girls sit and enjoy the ride, looking about at the closeness of the wildlife they are among. By the sides of the river banks, drifting silently by reedy clusters, there is much to discover that you would not see from the banks above. We as parents do all the paddling.

There is a lot of activity in the fields around us, which are mostly farmland. Cattle often come down to the river from the hot fields to enjoy a drink, but because of their weight and cumbersome frames as they tramp about, the ground between the banks and river becomes very muddy and swampy. I have been known to try to rescue cattle by the river in the past, when their feet have become waterlogged and stuck fast in the mud. But all you should do for them is to keep in your vessel, shout at them; 'Rah! Rah!' and bang about with the paddles. That is usually enough to scare the "stuck in the mud moos" and send them back on their way up the bank and into the fields.

As we carry on down the river, the sounds of distress come to our ears; the constant cries of a baby lamb which has strayed from its mother and fallen down the deep grassy bank to the river's edge. I can see another head peek out from the deep foliage of the bank. It is the mother, and she is close by her babe, showing such a devotion to her lamb that she cannot and will not leave it.

The girls are sorry for their plight, and we would not dream of passing them by. As we steer towards them, they look nervous and want to run, but there is nowhere for them to go, unless they climb back up. We all try to coax them, thinking that if one runs up the bank, the other will follow. Not so easy, as they are taking their time.

Then the decision comes to do the cattle roar. As we splash with paddles, instinct kicks in for our woolly friends. Suddenly the mother runs back up the bank in fright, and the baby lamb follows Mum in a hurry. Well that's our good deed for the day, and an experience for the girls in animal rescue techniques.

Soon after this we moor up and tie our canoe to the strong reeds that grow by the riverbank. We eat our sandwiches and drink our home-made lemonade by the river's edge, as Charlie and I earn some rest on the fair meadow, our bellies full and satisfied. The girls disappear into the long grasses in the fields behind us to play, and sit happily making necklaces out of buttercups. The children's joyful laughter, the warmth of the sun, the trickles of the river pass by, while buzzy bees' wings beat upon meadow flowers around our ears. Sunny days and memories forever.

As we come to, opening our eyes from our heavenly slumbers, rest time for us is over and it is time to get back on the river. Upon the river's gentle flow we stop again when approaching Goodrich Castle. I think the castle with its backdrop of forest trees looks good from this point, from the river bank. I take a photograph of the girls standing on the banks, with river and castle in the background. The draping withies beautifully frame the surrounding river grasses, all in the company of the pretty purple flowers of purple loosestrife.

As we push the canoe back into the river, much further on ahead, a jolly party of canoeists suddenly comes into view. The girls get quite excited because of the water pistols they are hiding in the bottom of the canoe. The unfortunate party of young people have their canoes tied together, and are chatting away and laughing as they paddle on.

We have just got past Lydbrook and are going on to Coldwell Rocks when we catch up with this party. I try to paddle fast by with a quick hello, as we know the tricks that are soon to begin. The girls' faces change from angelic 'butter wouldn't melt in their mouths' to naughty pixies. Having hidden flat in the canoe, they delightfully rise to the occasion, with devious looks to match, ready with their pump-action pistols, pointing at close range towards these unfortunates. Little horrors!

I was so embarrassed. When they discharged the pistols there were cheers of laughter from all on the river that echoed the valley that hot, humid summer's day. The canoeists were surprised to say the least, but they jollied along with what children do best – mischief. Such a drenching did these poor youths get that they might as well have jumped in the river. I did try to scramble up the river away from them as quickly as possible, but the pistols were more powerful than I had imagined, and squirted at long range. We apologised in motion when quickly passing, but thankfully they all saw the funny side of it, and thank god they did because they outnumbered us.

Later on we got to Symonds Yat East, where the other car was waiting, for us to load up and drive back to Hoarwithy. An extra night's camping, with a campfire as well, took us into Sunday morning, and it was time to return home.

As we took to the lanes back home, we travelled the silent small road through "hole in the wall", draped dark with trees in arched form within, and by woods to fields. Suddenly the tranquil silence was broken by an almighty din that echoed the air. The barks and howls of many hounds came out of nowhere, clearly on the trail of something good. The hounds were in formation packs, with noses firmly to the ground. They came all spilling out of the fields and were weaving about the land in a great frenzy, like ants from a disturbed nest. As they closed in down towards the river, the hounds never stopping their howling. They went down into the river, swimming confidently and with determination across the river's flow and on to the other side. Two men appeared to be supervising the chase, both waving their sticks in the air. They were both impeccably dressed for the occasion, in what looked like 1920s tweeds with britches and caps.

I felt sorry for that poor old Foxy Loxy, being chased by this gang of hounds. Perhaps, I thought, he was one of the regular culprits of this fair land, slyly inviting himself into the hen houses on his nightly raids, rudely disturbing those fat biddy chickens in the dark of the night. It seemed that this time he had counted his chickens before they had hatched. The game was now up for him, I thought, and I hoped he would get away. Others may not agree with me, and would ask how a townie like me would understand. But there is one thing I do feel, and always will - that this must be a rotten way to die. Although the fox must have been some way ahead of the hounds and on the other side of the river, I certainly would not like that lot on my tail. I still wonder to this day whether that old fox got away in the end.

All creatures great and small

All things bright and beautiful, the Lord God
made them all....

On the River Wye, in summertime gold
Came stories forth, made memories true
To creatures great, to creatures small
We tell the tale, her tales to you
Now they're imagined, for you unfold.

The river slow swirls thick as scum,
Stirs still the sunlights that we shared
And earthy stagnants, humid airs
Within the black shadows of Lydbrook.

She came to drink, but thirst was death
When life fell from the forest glades,
Where safe was home, born within shades
Lies a lifeless heap, on stinking riverbed
Beyond the black shadows of Lydbrook.

Then:
Camouflaged in summer, Coldwell Rock
At distance we came down approaching
Here men on river, with string and hook,
For salmon they had a plot for poaching
Within the shadows of Coldwell Rocks.

Shored up, we slid grey amidst the tender grass
He came into view supreme, appeared miraged,
Upon the waters, he mirrored pure on glass,
As if to embrace, his angelic wings of white,
Serene, alone strong, he was a swansong sight.

Emerged ashore graceful, with no fear, no fight
Stood tall towards us proud, at face to face
He then greedily took a snatched chocolate offering
As we fled to our vessel he gave chase
With his beastly hiss and orange beaky pecks
Our river friend now fell short of cherub in,
With dim halo hanging, miserable to his neck.

Then:
Onward; my little friends, I won't pretend to envy
Soars your freedom to the skies; there I admire
Watching fawn and feather, brings us together
Underneath the beautiful blazing planet on fire
My little friends, thine heart you mend, all of me.

Softly when I sleep in vessel and on rock
White lights make dazzled; soon they fade
For there you dance for me, above Wales blue
Then fall from me full into Earth's green glades
Where the calls of life once there were made.

Then:

Came along one afternoon, a swimming by
A grey squirrel paddling the width of Wye
With his tail chiffoned and kept afloat
Darting determined past my little boat
He cut the river sharp, to bank and tree
That he had eyed up at the other side
Ran like a skunk, arrowed wet up the trunk,
Where now, in foliage, squirrel happy hides.

Then:

Onwards to Monmouth, tiresome as we both know
There came a flitting turquoise from airs above
Paddled strides hard to chase, low afternoon sun,
A damsel beauty settled graceful on my glove.
For just a mile we talked, damsel hitched my ride,
While skimming the mermaid's hair and daisy fun
My little friend kept company with me by my side
Until beautiful he left, to withies and river's flow.

SABBATH SURPRISES

2004

One Sunday morning, I awoke from my slumber early to thoughts of not going to church today. It does not seem a good enough excuse not to attend church, but the waters of the Wye were beckoning to me from forty miles away. The weather was perfect for a paddle as we tied up our canoe on top of the truck. I just hoped with sly sideward glances that the pastor did not drive by, because the church is just up the road from my house.

Getting on our way off to the forest, I wanted to carry on straight through to Kerne, but Charlie wanted to stop for a coffee at Wilton Garage. The garage was busy, and so was the traffic out on the roads. While I waited for Charlie on the forecourt, he appeared with two coffees, to drink when we got to the start of our river journey. The beverages at Wilton are always guaranteed to be boiling hot, and their heat would last for the road journey, to be cool enough later to enjoy.

Charlie got into his truck and pulled out from the garage on to the roundabout, eventually getting away and speeding off into the traffic. I intended to take my turn to follow him and started to manoeuvre out of the forecourt, with all precautions taken. But as I proceeded, a manic horsebox driver steamed up beside me and tried to bolsh her way out in front of me to the roundabout. It was very plain to anyone that the driver of that horsebox was not looking in her mirrors at anything on the forecourt.

All I remember was the total disbelief at how close I was to getting crushed to death. The horsebox got closer and closer until the lorry caught the front of my truck and started to drag me out on to the manic roundabout. I beeped my horn frantically again and again to attract attention of the driver, but to no avail. As I continued to be dragged out on to the busy road, I could hear a very distressed horse inside kicking and neighing. There were a lot of diesel fumes as the driver revved for a quick exit, with me in tow.

While this was all happening, all I could think about was my father and how I needed him now, but he wasn't here any more. Then I realised that Charlie did not know what he had left behind on this forecourt, and what was happening to his wife. Then I thought - I have to deal with this. Just as I was about to climb over to the other seat and jump out of the passenger truck door, the lorry released my truck, but it took the headlights and bumper with it out on to the road.

So there I was, left in total shock, in limbo, half in and

half out of the forecourt. I was trembling and still in the escape position, but no one came to help me. I don't think they wanted to get involved. The horsebox sped off into the distance and I tried to memorise the number plate, but got only two letters. Manoeuvring my truck from the forecourt, I pulled desperately into a side road. After trying to collect my thoughts, I stepped out of the truck, not wanting to look at the damage. I felt a little sick at this unbelievable experience.

Then minutes later, the horsebox driver suddenly appeared there in the side road. She clearly knew she had done something wrong. Yet according to her I was in the wrong, and she wanted my details, because she was in a big hurry, looking at her wrist watch. I knew what I wanted to do to this scatty wench, but I did not have the strength to do it.

Then Charlie returned to the commotion. When the culprit had calmed down, we all departed each others' company, with insurance details exchanged. Charlie asked me if I wanted to continue our day's canoeing or return home, and I said nothing was going to stop me canoeing, so let's get on that bloody river. I don't know who was more bust up, me or the truck.

Arriving at Kerne, it was nice to get on the river at last. It preoccupied my mind, but I was canoeing today on my nerves. The day was spoilt, and our minds were on the incident at the garage. This stopped me from enjoying the scenery that I so love, and by the time I had got to Coldwell Rocks I was spitting feathers, with language to match. At least the rest of the day was kind to us, as was the River Wye with her soothing sounds, which calmed my mind a little.

We arrived at Symonds Yat East and tied the canoe up to have lunch on the riverbank. While we were eating a sandwich, a familiar voice on the upper pathway called down to us. We looked up to see our dear friend Roger, who we used to ride with in our motorcycling days, twenty-four years ago. Yes, it had been that long. Twenty-four years before we were in France, on motorcycles, crossing the border into Spain. We all met up in France and rode many miles for many days.

Roger still looked the same. We exchanged much conversation, as there was a lot of catching up to do. Roger still had his motorcycles, and had recently purchased a new canoe. It all seemed a strange day, with so much happening in it. We all made a date to meet up the following week and go on a canoeing trip together.

The coming weeks were consumed by form filling, road sketches and phone calls. I did have the upper hand on my case, because they had CCTV. When I asked them to forward me pictures, they did, which proved my case nicely.

FLOTSAM AND JETSAM

∾

EARLY SUMMER 2005

Coming towards Kerne Bridge, it is evident from the winters past how the levels of the risen water have pushed into the bridge all manner of debris. As we drift her waters, the river is as still as a millpond, looking like glass. Behind the reflections, through the arches of the bridge, rises up a yellow field of buttercups. When floating on the river, photographs are better, because you are on and within the river. I always remember when coming this way how Uncle Arthur scattered Auntie May's ashes from Kerne Bridge. So I always say 'Hello Auntie May, yet another stamp on the land from Charlie's family'.

As we approach the bridge, a woven mass of trees have knitted themselves tight on to the arches. All sorts are in there, including a few orange ring-shaped lifebuoys, iron gates, fence posts, and sometimes dead livestock. The mud carried through has dried thick and is now dusty, holding the debris high into the air, fixed. Under the bridge it is amazing to stall the canoe, in these calmer waters in summertime, and view underneath the engineering construction of the bridge.

Beyond this point from the bridge you have to have your wits about you, because the flow on this part of the river is very fast and curving. There is a small island of pebbles and withies which has formed over the years in the middle of the river (I mentioned this island earlier). It is advisable to keep right and steer carefully to avoid crashing into the bank of withies. This side is deeper, but the left side is shallow and stony.

MAGICAL TREES

2007

The golden years are yet to come, if it does not take me too long to visit woodland where veteran trees may still exist.

It grieves me to think of all that I have seen now, and all that I have missed. Even five to ten years can make a difference to the forest because of the natural falls of old trees and woodland clearing. In years past when I was busy canoeing up and down the river, and in the early days with my children, I never thought that in later years I would be hunting through the woodlands of the Forest of Dean to capture pictures of woodland life and write a book about it all. While I am fit enough to do it, all I want to do is share my experiences, and hopefully give future generations an appreciation of the vital need to keep this beautiful forest intact, educating my fellow humans that they need to keep and reap the benefits of the forests, for health of the mind, respect for their roots and sanity.

There can be some strange sights in the forest and some of amazing beauty, but it never ceases to surprise me how plants grow, and the extremes they will go to to survive.

Some reach great heights in the quest for light and cling to anything, growing and crashing into each other, ending up in many strange shapes as they head skywards, competing for the light. Even the trees' root systems grow spookily, lumped over themselves, and cover great stone walls and boulders as if poured from a jug like treacle. But you have to be adventurous to see these gems, and sometimes getting off the beaten track is the only way. It must be done with caution, because these trees are in the most awkward places, where no one ventures. It is mainly beeches that sprawl out creatively in these dark places of the woods, gripping their roots around anything to survive.

There is a tree with a sad face residing in Dennis Grove; I took a photograph of it before it could change. Not far from this place, by Leeping Stocks, is a deformed, stumpy tree which I named the mat tree. Its top is a fuzz of thin sticks sprouting out like a big old bad hairdo.

I soon found a mature beech which I photographed somewhere secret - I cannot disclose the location, but you may find it one day I hope. I can say we were on private land, and it was unsuitable to walk here. The trees are forgotten here and are not managed, and there are large holes in the ground which autumn leaves can cover up deeply. One great dip in the ground had barbed wire around it; maybe it had collapsed, as old mines do underneath, but we did stop and eat our lunch here, enjoying the company of the beautiful autumn leaves.

As we went on through the woods to the unknown, Charlie discovered it first. I could not believe the size of it. I ran to embrace its magnificence, falling at its feet in awe. Looking up to this giant of gnarled age, I saw that small knobbly growths were attached to its overhung branches, which were hanging gracefully back down to the earth, looking like rasta dreadlocks. The sun was low and burning orange in the distance over the other side of the Wye, which gave this old timer a sunset glow. As the sun set in the distance, its warmth disappeared, and the air became cold. It was getting late.

Before the day turned to dusk, I was on my knees taking a photograph of a tree we had discovered on the way out of the woods. Some people came towards us, shouting after a black labrador called Betty that had run on away from them. As they called the dog, she jumped on me, excited to see someone new.

At the foot of the trunk of the tree was a bracket fungus called hoof fungus, hard and brown and craggy like its host and shaped like an animal hoof (hence the name.) The fungus underneath was pale white in colour, and it sparkled as the low afternoon sun happened to place its last beams upon it. We had been in the right places at the right times to get the effects that the season had brought us that afternoon. It all seemed that this place was like a lost wood in a fairy tale book, and maybe it was.

BLUEBELL GIRLS

SPRING 2007

One spring afternoon on the banks of the River Wye, just a small way from Biblins Bridge, we all enjoyed a picnic. The girls passed time skimming pebbles across the river, the sunlight caught the splashes of water as the pebbles danced over its surface, and all was well with the trickling sounds of the softly-flowing river.

In Lords Wood the forest floor was adorned with bluebells, and the few oak trees still here were of good age. I took a photograph of one that spanned the width of three young ladies stood together, Kayleigh, Kiren and Daisymay.

Further into the woods the air became sticky and humid. Underneath the Seven Sisters Rocks, those limestone pillars which guard this part of the Wye, we ran with the girls in a game of hide and seek. Old fallen autumn leaves from the years before were deep and crisp as we all ran to hide from each other. Fresh young ferns crowded about our feet, and the colours of emerald shone from rich bouncy moss-lined root holes left by the fallen trees. The gentle flow of the Wye nearby drowned our laughter on this warm and scented spring afternoon.

Beauty be and beauty stay,
Captured our youth in springtime true
Scented our beginnings and children's play
With glowing cheeks, the shouts of joy,
Beneath our feet, the flowing tide
All running wild in emerald greens.
Our giant friends blend us away,
To weary hearts, and brows of sweat,
Upturns the earth, abounding we leapt,
Found us, its secret place, the hues of blues
With fleeting youths, for we can but hide,
Deep in our hearts you will be kept.

THE BANANA TREE

SPRING 2007

Rainfall and rivers had been high this year, even before the summer of this year's big rain and floods. From Kerne Bridge the path along the river was boggy to walk on, as the river had not long subsided, so we decided to climb up into Thomas Wood, away from the regular path.

Part of the railway era left behind became evident in the now-overgrown shrubbery of this wood. There was an old signal box, and through the shrubbery we saw old railway posts, tangled with wire and limply connected to the posts. The tunnel was quite small and partly blocked off. As we peeked into the darkness of the tunnel, water dripped fast through the brick roof. The air howled icy cold against our faces as it drove through from the other end of the tunnel, from the Lydbrook line. The temptation to take a torch and walk the tunnel was great, but it would have been a dangerous choice to make. The railway entrance had been bricked up so that people would not be tempted by their curiosity. These tunnels are so old now and not used, and they collapse. You could easily be buried alive exploring the tunnels.

A tiny cottage was discovered here well into Thomas Wood, built with large stones. The lintels above the window spaces can still be seen, and there is one single doorway. It has no roof, but inside a well-used fireplace was still intact.

Further on and out of the wood, we got back down to the drier path by the Wye. It was a long walk on to boggy grassland, boggier still where cattle had been grazing the year before. Teatime approaches, so we find a fallen oak tree that has sprawled out into the field and sit on the hard oak to enjoy the walnut and apple cake I had made the day before with a flask of tea.

Continuing the walk toward Bicknor, the land was changing out of its winter sleep, as April now was upon us. Catkins were hanging off the trees by the riverbanks, and strewn around the banks were straw bales dispersed from the fields up yonder, snatched away by the recent high waters and hanging untidily from the withies. It became apparent here that a swan was busy not too far from the waters, building a nest; she had taken advantage and gathered this material of straw. You could see that she was feeling rather confident as she attended her nest, arranging her newly laid eggs, turning them so gently before she sat again. We counted eight eggs, and she did not even know we were watching her.

The fields were waterlogged and it became tiresome to walk further, having to walk back again, but further on past Bicknor we did come across a strange tree. How it got to be that shape I will never know. It certainly looked a work of art, and from many angles. The two main branches attached to the trunk had split away on each side. You could see right through the tree to the other side, but how this split had happened is one of those mysteries of the forest. It had the appearance of a peeled banana, so that's the name we gave it - the Banana Tree.

A MOTHER'S LOT

JUNE 2007

This was a year no one will never forget. The rivers were already high in 2007, before the big flood of July emerged upon us.

One afternoon at 5 pm we travelled from Tewkesbury up the M50 to Symonds Yat, just to see how high the river was getting, as our own rivers, the Avon and the Severn, were spilling over. When we arrived we walked the path along the Wye. The river was very high and very noisy, and Charlie held out his phone to record the rush and tumble of the weir.

A little further up the path, my eye caught a white bundle on the other side of the river. Upon closer inspection I could see that it was a mute swan who had laid her eggs on this little bit of an island before the swollen river had come. The swirling torrent was soon to engulf her and her eggs. This sorrowful sight made me want to cry, as I so much appreciated her determination as a mother to ensure the survival of her babes in their shells, keeping them warm as she curled up tight upon them and wished for the waters to reside.

We returned a week later, when the river looked no better. We could see that the swan had had no choice but to bail out, because her island had all but disapeared. Perhaps it was better this way, for if the cygnets had come into the world they would have been swept away and suffered for it. Sadly for a great many birds on the river, ground nesters and tree dwellers, the floods would have been fatal. In my own town in Tewkesbury I remember down by the old mill some moorhens were nesting in the reeds, as they had done every year for as long as I could remember. To them this year were born five chicks, little black balls of fluff so sweet and squeaky, and I knew their fate as the waters came upon us like Noah's flood - it was all so quick. And human mothers did not escape either. Hence my story to you: "A Mother's Lot".

A year has come to great despair
Our little ones are all but lost
To raging torrents of rivers curse
When Nature took its timely cost.

Stay with our broods we tried in vain
But no mercy the waters had for us
Swept our babes away upon the tide,
This mother's lot, to feel the pain.

AFTERMATH OF
THE FLOODS

SEPTEMBER 2007

July 2007 was the time when the great floods came and went
for us in the UK. It is now September, and autumn has
arrived, with the calm after the storm. Having been born in
Tewkesbury and lived there all my life, I thought I would
just be another descendant of my ancestors, who saw flood
devastation down the ages in this town, as my ancestors
came from the Norman Conquest, settling here in
Tewkesbury in 1066.

People back then had a few more fields for the spilling of
a swollen river to spread into. The worst losses affecting
them would have been their livestock, their livelihoods,
which to them would be like losing your house now, and
back then there was no insurance for them to fall back on.

There was no end of work for us for the next two years,
because of the desperate climate. Our trade of ceramic tiling
meant that we were the last to come into a building or house
after other works had been completed, to tile the walls and

floors. People were crying out for our services, just so they could get back to some normality and back into their homes. This was our gain financially, though we worked full hammer to help everyone we could, but the sadness and stories still remained of the losses. Sedgeberrow seems to stay with me, as it was very bad down there. We worked all hours for four families, all related, and it was all down to us, which made you feel quite responsible. Early mornings became late nights, and weekends as well.

The waters had risen to within less than an inch of each of these houses' ceilings. The extra waters had come from a nearby brook which ran through a cul de sac. The brook could not take the volume of rainwater and had spilled over and gushed through the gardens at speed. On top of this a nearby wheatfield which came close to the houses rushed rainwater from the top of the field, meeting the brook's spill below. All the growing wheat was dragged out of the field, bringing the wheat home in a different sense. The mess and loss were unbelievable.

A friend of ours, a carpenter from the same village, had a young family. He told us how he had looked out at his back garden to see what looked like a dam bursting. The water was rushing fast and unstoppable towards his house. He had nowhere to run and no time to do anything except to get the family upstairs. A customer in the same village said that his outdoor jacuzzi had come loose, as the waters had pushed through the gardens and uprooted the bolted-down jacuzzi. He and his neighbours had to wade after the jacuzzi, up the lane, but it was all to no avail, as the waters whisked it away to unknown pastures new, I laughed when he told us, wondering where the bath had ended up.

Total misery visited many in the county, and everyone will have a story to tell, for years to come, for the history books. The loss of a young life came hard for us Tewkesbarians. A nineteen-year-old boy called Mitchell who was in my daughter's class at school tried to cross a small road bridge where the water from the Swilgate Brook was raging past the abbey. He never made it, paying the ultimate price for wanting to get home. Everyone knew him and his family well. He was a talented student and was going places, according to Frankie, our dear friend. Mitchell was found a week later, when the waters receded.

Two other men of Tewkesbury lost their lives here, in the same location, at the rugby club. I needed to talk of these three men in my book, and to honour their memory to our brothers of Tewkesbury.

★　★　★　★　★

Well autumn is here and we are canoeing on the Wye. We are approaching Lydbrook, and the old railway bridge that crosses the river here. When the children were small I named this bridge Oildrum Bridge, because it is big and black. Water marks can be seen half way up its legs, and I am surprised it is still standing.

Everything around us is covered in dried dusty mud, right

up to the banks and over. The risen waters of July carried through everything imaginable and dumped it. It never ceases to amaze me how these bridges stand the forces of the river when she comes raging through, with the volume of water and the tons of weight pushing hard up against them. Their safety might become a cause for concern one day.

Down against the middle leg of the bridge, it becomes apparent that a green canoe has been swiped from somewhere upriver and carried down towards Lydbrook, where it rests shoved into one of the bridge's supports. It looks quite funny, as it has been moulded and wrapped tight around the support. The force of the high water was enough to keep the canoe pinned there. As I approach the bridge close up I take a picture of it, bent and twisted and almost turned inside out.

Later on in the day our trip takes us down towards Monmouth, where we pass the weir at Symonds Yat. Further on down the river, past the withy island, and on the right hand side of the river, lies the lush land at Wyestone Leys. As we continue our tranquil journey, we are suddenly disturbed by two very rough and dirty-looking young men who appear at the side of us, splashing out from the banks. They continue to wade the width of the river in front of us, plastic bin liners slung over their backs to keep whatever is inside them dry. I do not like the look of them, and their behaviour seems strange, so I tell Charlie to give them a wide berth in case they have been watching us come down the river. They might be on the run from somewhere, or they might even want to rob and attack us. Well my paddle is ready mate, and they will get it if any funny business starts. We do not give them a chance, as the river's flow and our own efforts carry us on and out of harm's way.

Our trip today is good, but it's a bit of a dirty one. Everything along the way looks wrecked and flat. Filth is dominant all along the river. Towards Monmouth, some plum trees are growing in rows along the river, hanging close over the waters. The bottoms of the trees are covered in thick muck where the waters came up so high, but the trees' bounty of fat ripe plums still grows heavy out of their mucky, battered, half dead leaves. But soon enough all the leaves of the forest will fall, and the rains and snows of winter will come, and the springtime will emerge once more and announce a new birth, waking the forest and river up again, fresh and new.

FAREWELL TO
AN OLD FRIEND

⤳

SPRING 2008

Along the stretch of river where we go canoeing is a piece of
land just off the main road, the B4234 through Bishopswood.
This land is fertile, wild and beautiful with meadow fare.
Here many different species of trees stand apart from each
other, including an old English oak and a veteran to this place
close by the river. The oak is well established, and stands just
a stone's throw from the river bank.

We had ten years of our lives canoeing past our old friend
on the bank and admiring the oak's seasons. 2007 was a
colourful autumn for our old friend, and I took a glorious
bronze and deep orange-leaved photograph of it from my
canoe. I was unaware that this would be his last show.

One spring Sunday afternoon in 2008, we were canoeing
this way. The afternoon was bright, and the tranquil river
was like a millpond. As we drifted with effortless speed
down the river, Charlie lay down in the canoe, dangling his
hands in the waters, while I steered gently with my paddle

to keep the canoe from turning in a circle. I looked over to our old friend as we approached the land where he stood, but he was nowhere to be seen. All we could see was a broken shell of a tree and a vacant space. This was unexpected, and it was with sadness that we realised the end had come.

We were in no doubt that we had been privileged to see this old oak at its finest in our lifetimes, as he must have been a few hundred years old. Our dear old friend had fallen back into the land he had come from, hollow and outlived.

We gently paddled across the river and moored the canoe on to strong river weed that grew from the side of the bank. Walking across this piece of land, we were the first to step through all the fresh meadow fare of grasses and buttercups and wild flowers. Upon reaching the oak we saw that its wide heavy head had fallen backwards, breaking off from the gnarled stumpy trunk. Charlie stood inside the hollow of the oak, revealing its massive size - you could fit four men inside the trunk of this tree. I broke some of its bark away to keep, and will put it in a frame for the wall back home, a gift from our dear old friend.

A poem came to me from the tree, and it went like this.

Beside the Wye in pastures green
My beauty grew within your soil
All seasons past, I have felt and seen
God's creatures rested on my hair

A weary soul my sleep not spoiled.
For now my life is at an end
No more the seasons I will share
Depart with sorrow l won't pretend
My shells forlorn, and laid all bare,
Farewell
Farewell.

VANISHED
CONGREGATIONS

❧

APRIL 2008

St Margaret's Church at Welsh Bicknor is much like the church at Hoarwithy, though plainer. It has decorative stonework with built-in pillars, still beautifully intact. This church was built in 1858 and once served a large population from the surrounding estate, but it is largely empty these days. Worshippers used to cross the Wye by hand ferry to attend services here at St Margaret's, but now all is quietly vacant. I look to the church and say - bring her back into the fold of worship once again. I wonder whether the Church of England could do something for this church. I know everything is money and has to be worth running these days, but surely not to be left to rot back into the woods. It would be a shame to lose this gem of the forest.

The front porch of St Margaret's houses the heavy wooden doors to the church, padlocked with strong chains. When I peeped through the large keyhole I almost expected to see an old-time congregation of people, but cold emptiness ruled, revealing a faded and threadbare carpet leading up to the altar. Vacant dusty pews were seated each side of the church, once warm with the throng of the congregation but now silent. The sun shones through a side window, sending sunbeams streaming towards the altar as if to beg a priest to awaken the church from its sorry state. The air coming through the keyhole carried a stale and musty, cold and dusty aroma. I imagined the echoing of prayer and sermon and the songs of yesteryear, voiced by a community which had long passed away to the graveyard outside.

These people who lived, worked and worshipped here at Welsh Bicknor no doubt now lie here in their resting places, some recently buried. Older headstones have sunk into the ground with time, crooked and buried within the strangling couch grasses. Lichen covers the inscribed names, which are fast disappearing in these times of acid rain. The headstones still bear the faint inscriptions of some of the sweetest words of the age. My eyes well up with emotion as if I know them personally when I read such heavenly verse. And many of them are so young, often just children.

The angelic carved faces and flowers upon these stones are the simple but skilled stonework of the time, and part of me feels disrespectful at stepping on their graves, even though it is not deliberate. I jot down the ages and names and sweet verses of belief, the comforting words inscribed upon the tombs by the departed for their friends. There is the faint inscription of a rope-carved gravestone by the back church door, of a young boy who drowned aged sixteen and rests here. It reminds me sorrowfully of a recent loss to my own town in Tewkesbury, where a young man of nineteen drowned. The same rivers in any age can take us from life.

Labour's done, 'tis past the week
This sabbath day of wanted rest
To serve our Lord and look our best.
The children play and mothers scold,
Up to the path, leads to the door
And waiting by porch, out in the cold
Priest's greeted hand, we all sit inside
The holy place where prayers reside
With voices raised heavenward in song
Our souls are cleansed, this day belongs.

SUMMER HUNTERS

~

In the summertime the Sister Rock is a beautiful armchair of peace and tranquillity. All around are the breath-taking views to a never-ending expanse of forest and skyline; you really feel on top of the world. Here upon this rock it feels a privilege to be at one with nature as we enjoy watching the peregrine falcons command the air space above us. Their territory and nest sites are nearby, over from the rock we stand upon.

When the babes have left the nest, we watch the young fly off from their nesting site, swooping back and forth from rock to rock within the small familiar space. They are preparing their wings for flight, and to gain their confidence, like a toddler getting up on his feet for the first time. The expressions on these young birds' faces as they perch safe from awkward landings is quite funny. They look back up to the parent as if to say, "I've done it Daddy!" It pulls at the heartstrings and brings a lump in the throat.

We have experienced the peregrines' feeding times, having waited patiently and long. As the young falcons wait in the safety of a secluded ledge, suddenly excitement breaks out when father brings the food home. By this time the young are bigger than the parents. And as time goes by, which only seems like weeks, the peregrine falcons take their children to the skies.

One afternoon when Charlie and I were enjoying the summer sights upon the rock, a peregrine parent with two young came into focus in the sky above us. Today was the day for flying lessons. As we watched how the parent dived and swooped through the skies with the young, encouraging them in every way. It was a wonderful sight. It was as if they were saying "You are up here now and you have to get on with it", and that is just what the young falcons did.

From ugly white fluffy birds with big yellow eyes
They emerged perfect from a ledge nest
Feathers all new, proud in perfect forms,
Skilful they became, in flight at their best
Into a world with sun, rain and storms
Peregrine falcons outweigh the rest;
They are the masters of the forest skies.

★ ★ ★ ★ ★

Buzzards are another favourite with me. They are so graceful as with no effort they climb the thermals, or cruise gently on them as their heads swivel around in mid air, scouring the forests below. They can drop out of the sky at any moment with folded wings and gathering speed, then they regain their composure and return immaculately to stable flight.

There are a fair few buzzards in this area, and I am beginning to think that these birds of prey are getting more plentiful. Binoculars are a good tool to scour the forest ahead. There is a tall stumphead of a dead tree on the other side of the river, in the forest of "far harkening rock". As I look through the glasses, I can see that this tree serves as a rest and lookout perch for a buzzard.

This part of the forest has been partly cleared, leaving bare space between fallen trees. Its slopes reveal deer trying to manage the heights to the lower secluded forest below to graze upon new shoots. There are many species of tree on this side of the forest, and all their tops look a different shade of green, which in autumn looks stunning with variations of bronze, yellow and orange.

Looking almost straight over the river from this point, up towards the top edge of the forest, a good-looking stag appears with his ladies. He moves down the slopes, very carefully out of the woods and into the open. He leads the way and the ladies follow. The stag has quite a harem with him, and we watch with delight as they gently graze.

Down on the river below us, the laughter of canoeists can be heard, travelling towards Monmouth. Aluminium canoes make a racket as their paddles clank against the sides all up the river. You can see the wet paddles catching the sunlight like glinting mirrors shining back up at you.

In the middle of the river going on to Monmouth is a little island which has built up over the years, rooted in withies and making a withy island. Here a pair of swans nest every year, with only a few ducks in residence sharing. When we pass down this part of the river in our canoe, we often get a hiss and lurching of necks from these swans, so we keep our distance, which is difficult because the bank and the withy island have become closer over the years with caught debris.

The water here to the left has a faster flow, so we are not in the swans' feathers for too long. If you paddle on the right side of the river, you will get stuck in the river weed, as over the years it has built up. So if you don't want to "canoe a carpet", specially when the weed is in flower, keep to the left side of the river, otherwise the swans might get you.

THE RUNAWAY
HARVEST

◠

AUGUST 2008

Early morning views from Wilton Bridge looking up to Ross show us the wide expanse of the River Wye. The rising waters curb the corners of the river towards us at speed, commanding its forces against the bridge's structure. Nothing gets away from its grip and nothing gets in its way as waters scoop everything up, anchored or not, dead or alive, slamming all matter into it as it rages by and onwards to the sea.

Driving on up the A40 I look to the left, where a golden field is already harvested. A few large round bales are placed to the middle of the field, as the farmer has already taken precautions by moving his stock away from the river's edge. The Wye has clearly risen further and is level now with his field. It looks scary as you can see it spilling up over the banks from the water's edge, crawling slowly towards the golden harvest.

Later on, after a good afternoon's walk through the

forest, we take a rest on one of the Sister Rocks before going back home. The river down below from this point, so high up, looks wild. Then to our surprise, in the distance, we see a flotilla of half-submerged bales floating down the river. They drift towards us in perfect formation one after the other. The bales look familiar, and I wonder if these are the same ones I saw from the A40, threatened by the rising waters, and they have been scooped out of those fields by the river's snatching drag. Could it be, I thought, that the river had risen rapidly enough to take away the farmers' bales we had seen earlier? It was possible, as it had been about a couple of hours before.

Looking down at the river below through the binoculars, I can see that a crafty crow has landed on one black-wrapped bale, and is contently hitching a ride on it downriver to Monmouth. Perhaps it is quicker and more relaxing to sail there than to fly.

On returning back home along the A40, we glance over to the field with the bales in that we had passed earlier in the day. The golden harvest is all but gone. The river has indeed claimed most of the bales, and it was they we saw floating by underneath the Sister Rock. The edges of this field now reveal a regimental line of floaters ready to go off down river at any moment.

What a shame - all the farmers' hard work, time and money wasted, and all that summer sunshine to grow the crop. For months afterwards, as we continued to travel the A40, these bales remained a sprawling mess, dragged out of shape, damaged and useless, left all over the fields' edge. I think the farmer lost heart and thought, it can all stay there now.

Throw the seed, new birth shall provide
Where river's edge is neighboured near
As nature kind as turned her upper hand
Then our harvest ready, came ours to fear,
All toils spoiled, speeds the water upon this land,
Now slips me many a penny through fingers,
Sneers authority passing, to a hole in the pocket,
Snatches away a prime winter bounty,
When passing through the golden county.

KINGDOM OF THE WILD BOAR

∾

OCTOBER 2008

It was a blustery Sunday afternoon in Doward as we walked through the woods. Strange forest sounds filled the air and danced on the winds. They disappeared again, only to be carried back to our ears again within seconds.

We knew what they must be – wild boar. We had never experienced the sounds of the boars before, yet today there seemed to be many of them, and so close. I was apprehensive but excited that I might be lucky today in getting some photographs of these animals.

Charlie and I decided to take on another Sister Rock next door from the other point we sit on, but this one was harder to get on to. We had to hold on to old yew trees that grew into its sloped forest bank. It was a slippery and muddy climb down to get on to the rock ledge. This location is quite secluded and is not used, as few people attempt to come to this rock.

Once on the narrow rock ledge the panoramic view can

be seen differently from another vantage point. We sat for half an hour upon this rock listening to the wild boars' grunts somewhere below us. At times, because the day was windy, the wind carried these grunts much further.

Suddenly we heard some foraging close by with the sounds of grunts in quick succession. It all sounded so scary because here we were in the seclusion of the forest, and not really on safe ground. I had heard these boars can be a bit moody and charge at you, and a picture began to grow in my imagination.

Upon this narrow piece of rock with great drops below, we found an opening through the shrubbery that led to a grassy ledge. We managed this by coming down on our bottoms to a lower ledge, while holding tight on to twisted tree branches that grew out of the rock face. There was room enough for us to sit here for a while and have a sandwich and a cup of tea. The winds continued to howl around us within the forest, this other world deeper. Looking to the lower path, the sounds of grunts were ever nearer, and I began to feel a bit scared, and then really scared, because we were out of our territory. Perhaps if we kept silent for a while here and ate our sandwiches, the boar might just trot along the path underneath our dangling feet, and still be a safe distance away. There was a big drop below us, but it was not too difficult to manage the steep flat rock face down. Then I thought to myself - are we mad to be this curious, and possibly risk falling? I might add that safety ropes were not needed, although it sounds crazy.

Once we were down on this path, tiny but walked well by animals, the rocks that in time had fallen from the rock face were buried in the autumn leaves, and they rolled under our feet when we were trying to get a firm footing. In all the time we were there, the sounds of the boar continued, sounding just as close. There were also many trotter imprints between the mud and leaves along this path, and upon checking them we knew they were not the prints of deer. I felt threatened and somewhat scared, and I will admit, I wanted to scarper.

As we neared a corner around the rock face, I wondered what I would do if the boar had occupied this area. But they were nowhere to be seen. Part of me was glad, but only part. All that remained in front of us now was a large overhang of rock. It could have been good shelter for man or beast, and as it was, it became clear that both man and beast had stayed there lately. Coarse hair could be clearly seen strewn about the ground within this sheltered rock, which made it clear that the wild boar had been staying here. There was also a strong domestic pig aroma about the place.

A few metres away we saw the place where a fire had been prepared and lit a long time ago. The remaining unburned wood in the fire had turned to dust.

Further on around the rock face was a strange hole, and inside this hole was a formation of a smaller rock. If this was a natural occurrence of the movement of rock, I would say it could be a good art piece. When coming into these untamed areas of forest I do have the urge to get back to my roots, so I began to chisel away at the rock, creating an image of my canoe with a bird of prey circling above it, and signing it 'DDFS 2008'. True it is that we do still feel the need, no matter how civilised we think we are, to put the "flint to the rock".

4 pm was approaching and dusk was creeping in. The wind was still whipping up, the trees above were swaying and the grunts of the wild boar were still sounding. Charlie looked at me, and our thoughts were the same: the coming night was drawing in, and we were both convinced that these piggies were coming home to rest for the night, back to the coarse hair bed under the rock overhang where we still were. We did not relish the thought of meeting up with unknown numbers of these wild beasts. Nor did we want to be uninvited guests to this pongy piggy abode, so it seemed a good idea to depart. Well that's it then, no pictures today Deb, those secretive little porkers weren't going to show up, and it was getting dark.

As we hurried along the piggy path and back up to the civilisation of the 21st century that awaited us, I wondered for a moment why fifty-year-olds were doing what twenty-year-olds might not. But alas, human curiosity dies hard, with the chance of a photograph, It's another world down here, and it's worth taking risks for these old mysteries of the forest.

Steeply now and onwards down
Into the depths of their forest world
Dancing grunts are upon the wind
As we leave behind the sisters' crown
Our narrow walk along piggy's path,
Twists around the feet of Sister Rock,
They will soon return, homeward bound
To rest their tired piggy trots.

QUARRY'S EYE

～

SUMMER 2008

There are many quarries in the Forest of Dean, but this one is special to us for more than one reason. Once discovered you cannot keep away from Doward; it seems to have magnetic psychological forces that play on my mind when I am away from it. For me it is so ancient here that I feel it deeply in all its seasons. A walk through Doward woods drops down by twisty paths, in three directions made by man, while one path is made by animals and is narrow and arched by brambles, secluded and secret. We have taken them all. Paths in this wood lead away from each other in different directions, all to meet at the same location, on the bottom path into Lords Wood.

On one path by the quarry, the ground underfoot becomes rocky upon descent and is kissed richly in places by a spongy emerald green moss, while the byways of the path are adorned with bright wild miniature strawberries which intermingle the pathway. So tiny are these strawberries that I'm sure they are a welcome juicy forest fare for animals' tiny mouths in season.

Multitudes of wild flowers are abundant here in their season too; red, pink and white valerian, common knapweed, self heal, bugle, scabious, hemp agrimony, speedwell, perforate St John's wort. Wild dog roses and travellers' joy hang in canopies over the draping beeches down to the quarry's gate.

Oak and beech live close beside each other, while within these mature beeches that adorn the entrance down into the quarry's eye, the hot sun above filters through the green glades with a dappled light that forever change the picture, and the gentle warm breeze flows through, making the trees move. Peregrines live here within these carved rocks of old, discovered this year.

Lead me down your mossy path
Laced rich with strawberry fare
Where beeches reach up into the sky
Caress unknown steps along the way,
Deep down into the quarry's eye.

Quarry, place of home, where babies sleep,
Upon the wing, brought into life
Faithfully to your rocks sure they keep,
The guarded brood on quarry's height.

Man of the woods

There in the forest, along the Dowards' way,
Through shady trees of leafy glade
We met a man of woods called Mike

Friendly was he, with his forest mates
For strangers were we, by Quarry's Gate;
This man of woods, he welcomed us in,
Told stories of his, he trusted us true
For there we loved all the same thing,
Friendship was made, as laughter grew.

There in the forest,
Along the Dowards' way,
Through shady trees of leafy glades
Our friend was there, now rides a bike
All on his own down by Quarry's Gate;
Here came a stranger, but not a mate,
He is not trusted true, not welcomed in
The stranger he did clap his hands,
For he with us, loved not the same thing,
Friendships not made, this volunteer clan.

There was once in the forest, along the Dowards'Way,
Through shady trees of leafy glades
The man of woods, he is not there
He absent be, down by Quarry's Gate;
For the stranger now is on the rocks,
She is not there, no babes, no mate,
Unwelcomed foe, untrusted flew
Once here a gem within the forest fare
Were stories gold and friendship true,
We love the same thing, the same as you,
With friends and birds came all to share.

This is a poem to a man called Mike who we met in the forest when we first started to walk Doward in 2008. He was a lovely forest man, and a real man of the woods. He was dedicated to his pastime, in the forest with the deer, and the birds of prey. He spent many hours watching them and watching out for them. He cared deeply about the forest, and was full of stories. He accepted and trusted us, and let us use his equipment to view the birds of prey.

Mike really made me laugh when he told me of a time he had been in the forest waiting for hours, in a proper hide, to see these deer. He took a drink from a can in his bag and pulled the ring on the can, realising too late that the deer were very near his hide. The deer heard the 'psst', which he could not muffle, and ran away.

NO MAN'S LAND

AUTUMN 2008

Clearing operations at Little Doward woods inspired this
title, and yes it really does look a barren piece of land now.
The ground here has been gutted, and it looks as if there
has been a war here. There are massive holes where once
tree roots grew which look as if shells have hit, and trees
which look as if their tops have been blown off. The former
forest floor has been reduced to a deep and spongy feeling
underfoot. This is where the bodies of trees have been
shredded to a pulp, and in places you will sink up to your
knees. One massive beech had fallen flat over, and all
because the ground here was too pulpy to support its roots.
It proved that all trees in woods to some extent support each
other. These mature beeches and oak trees at Little Doward
had been unsympathetically felled and shredded by
machine.

I do feel somewhat deprived at not having discovered this
beautiful wood sooner. All this was to make way for grazing
land, and what permission, I thought, did they have to
destroy this ancient land so ruthlessly? And could they, the

powers that be, have chosen a pine wood instead for animal grazing? Habitat and history and educational purposes were taken away in hours, compared to the centuries it took to produce this jewel in the crown. Preservation orders and good management of woods - where are they?

Along this way in Little Doward remains a veteran uncoppiced beech pollard. This crooked old man of the woods has grown at a slant and is gnarled in all kinds of shapes. Full of years, it almost has a face, which if it could talk would tell you a hundred stories. Growing on this beech is a fungus that looks like a trumpet, named the chanterelle. This fungus is found on broadleaved trees (eg beech, oak and birch).

GIANTS OF SILVER

～

OCTOBER 2008

It was a wild windy Sunday afternoon in late October.
Walking up the steep lane at Little Doward, autumn was in
full swing, and many leaves had already scattered the forest
floor. Underfoot along our path into the woods were
hundreds of beetles, too many to count, crawling about the
fallen leaves. We gingerly tiptoed through the deeply-laden
forest, hoping not to step on any of these busy little beetles.

On reaching the deeper parts of Doward, we saw that
timber operations and the clearing of land had left their
mark. The land about looked ravished, torn and split,
squashed and flattened, sawn and battered. A few large
stumps were visible within the deep mulch, and I wondered
why these trees had not been preserved. I was frustrated to
think of the big old trees that I had missed. I was too late,
and won't experience that growth again in my lifetime.

My attention was attracted to the lower land as I saw in
the distance the stark image of what looked like the
skeletons of silver giants. Standing on higher ground, and
looking down at the distant backdrop of wooded area, these

107

mature beeches were magnified to the eye and were in
spectacular form. I felt I could hear their words ringing true.

In times of old we were born in our place
A forest fruit, saplings did rise
The glory days of seasons past.
Among the living, here we stand
Elements to break us, we despise
Naked and grey we await our fate
Back in the earth will lie our waste.

TUMULUS

OCTOBER 2008

One Sunday afternoon in October, we walked together through Long Chase Wood. The woods were moving with the high winds, which further blew away the autumn leaves golden through the earthy airs, yonder and beyond more than a drop from a tree. Throughout the forest between cave and rock the wood had become a fire of colours.

Charlie walked on ahead, leaving me alone for a while. As I closed my eyes and rooted myself still, I began to breathe the forest in deeply. And it was here the forest moved with me. True I felt the buffeting airs that were cast my way, upon my face and body, and for peaceful moments I was at one with the woods. As I came to from my dreamy moments alone, I began to walk to an upper pathway, and soon came to a ledge. I looked further over the edge to see that the drop was deep. Bracing myself against strong winds so high up, the explosion of fireworks came to my eyes. There in the depths below, the wet black-barked smooth beeches, these majestic trees of old, grew from the craggy rocks of limestone. Their branches reached up towards me like a giant black octopus, and hence these branches of reaching arms came to me smothered in Nature's finest colours. As I looked down at my feet, my legs were getting tangled with the ledge's brambles, which held me back safely. I could not permit myself to see more, as in a tranced stare my head became a whirl. I was dizzy with the forest's beauty. In all that the forest had to offer, drawing me in closer, to feel all senses, to everything it was to be alive, I sent a poem to my love.

Stood upon the pathway ledge,
brambles twinning around my legs
I tilt my body to the edge,
Into the deep and heavenly realms,
Bursts orange, yellow, bronze and browns.

Naked I fall into your space
Stripping colours away, that cushion dreams,
Below, the mossy rocks, and bouncy earth
Bury me deep within the forest's place.
For you I love so very much,
Consumed by your scents,
Caressed by your touch.

Look up! Giants of silver, reaching high,
Where the bird of prey circles its flight,
In your never-ending truest sky.

Ganarew CP Tumulus: I felt myself being absorbed, and digested, into the nature of it. Hence, upon this moment in time, I gave my soul to her.

'Mermaid's hair' (water crowfoot) on the Wye

Messing about on the river

The *Wye Invader*

Memorial to a drowned boy, Coldwell Wood

Fields of yellow – buttercups near Coldwell Rocks

Bluebells at Doward

A ferry boat reclaimed by nature

Hoof fungus near Dennis Grove

Giant oak tree in Lords Wood with Kayleigh, Kiren and Daisymay

Veteran beech

Giant beech at Leeping Stocks

The 'banana tree' near Bicknor

A mother's lot - swan on her nest at Symond's Yat in high water

A canoe swept against the railway bridge at Lydbrook

Beeches at Wyestone

Veteran beech at Wyestone

Our old friend the oak near Bishopswood, before the fall

An old friend fallen

St Margaret's Church, Welsh Bicknor

The quarry at Doward

Looking for Bigfoot, Staunton

Beechwood beauty

Golden beech, early autumn

Fallen beech in 'no man's land'

The quarry at Doward

Snow scene at Doward

Snow on Biblins Bridge

Misty vista near Goodrich

Badger sett near Coppit Hill

Bluebells in Cadora Woods

The shell of an old building at Park Wood, Welsh Bicknor

Primroses in Park Woods

Cadora Woods – bluebells and wild garlic

Cadora Woods, looking over to Penallt

Bees' nest, Pwllplythin Woods

Foxglove avenue

Charlie's mum in Foxglove Avenue

Ancient chestnut, Joint Wood

Young caterpillars attack a beech leaf, Doward

Ancient yew at penallt church

Winter wonderland at Doward

Rescue from the floods near Redbrook

Under the railway bridge at Lydbrook

The flooded river at Redbrook

The railway bridge at Redbrook

Beech tree at High Meadow

Great mullein at Long Close Wood

Abandoned hut in the woods at Hendre

Timber truck at Hendre

Tricholoma mushrooms by the river at Lordswood

Our boys, Monmouth

Dymock gold

St Mary's Church, Kempley

Autumn beeches near Birchen Wood

The oaks' graveyard

TEA WITH THE FAIRIES

NOVEMBER 2008

Walking down through by Lordswood, the late afternoon sun heralded the forthcoming winter chill. The sun illuminated the backdrop of autumn colours, which magnified the Seven Sisters Rocks, peaking out like white beacons bathed in this autumn glory.

Beside the river we strolled along into the woods. Close by the path lay a fine green mossy log, damp and deep within the undergrowth. It owned many lovely cream-coloured cups of bracket fungus, which grew undisturbed and in perfect in form. To me they looked like fairy cups from a fairytale in a book I knew when I was a child. Captured in these fungus cups was a fine collection of fallen ash, oak and beech leaves, taken by the winds to their place of rest.

This wonderful sight in all its colours rolled away, hidden within the undergrowth by the Wye, stirring the child in me. It is true to say that the forest has a way of taking you back into your childhood. When entering the woods anywhere, I always secretly revert back to being a child, as I never feel grown up here, not even for a moment. The forest will always be revealing her never-ending treasures for you to discover if you look carefully, and you will feel amazement and delight when you find them.

At this moment in time by the mossy log, my imagination was set to the "fairies' tea party" which comes but once a year. And if you are lucky enough to be on this path at this special time of year, be you man or beast, one of you will dine with the fairies at their mossy log table, laden with the most charming cups of nature's finest nectar.

Dine with us now this autumn day
A crimson fare, please come and share
Tis once only in a year, our sups,
You chosen one along this way,
Be seated at our charming feast,
Sit up! Sit up! Man or Beast,
Drink deeply into our fairy cups.

SNOWDRIFTS

FEBRUARY 2009

From Tewkesbury we arrived again at Doward. It is a place that was familiar, but here and now, the deep snows made this place look unfamiliar and unknown. There was silence, for no one else had ventured out. Even the birds had disappeared, not one to be seen or heard. The snow had caressed the forest, giving the air freshness, with that special scent that only new snow can give. One could hear one's own heartbeat within this mysterious silence, and the beauty of being the first to touch the new-laid snows, which with a million sparkles glints to the eye, when the sun casts beams of light upon the snows surface, made a memory forever.

The skies turned to grey and the warmth of a blizzard drifted in. Distant forest trees very quickly disappeared in a veil of white, and we moved down with it into the shelter of woods towards the old quarry. The pressure was on as the heavy blizzard came upon us. It was hard to breathe as the blizzard came across in force. The snowflakes were as big as two-pence pieces and there really was nowhere to hide. The sparse trees, already heavy laden, became blobs on the landscape. I think it was a case of the drifting snows sticking to branches and twigs and then freezing solid as the next lot came in on top.

Charlie shielded my camera to keep the lens dry, which was a bit of a fight as the blizzard came in at an angle. I did manage to capture some pictures while holding my breath in the heat of the moment, of the blizzard against the grey rocks of the old quarry. We then went down deeper into the woods, which gave us shelter at the foot of these giant beeches, for the action was still happening above the tree tops. The air within the forest of trees became warmer, as underfoot along a path unrecognised our feet crunched into the untouched snow. It all became another world with the complete silence. I felt lost already, no movement, no breeze, no birds, just breath and silence. Every twig, no matter how small and thin, was piled high, flakes upon flakes of perfect snow. Nothing fell, all was living and sleeping and frozen beautifully as if caught in a fairytale book.

We came out on to the Sister Rock upon which we had enjoyed so many summer days. Out in the open here, and so high up, the blizzard was still drifting across. Nothing around was recognisable, and it looked like just another rock. The sky was dirty grey and looked as dark as night was falling soon. Our two bodies standing alone on this rock made me feel for a moment as if we were the only people in the world, lost within the mists of time. The volume of forest far and wide, to and beyond Biblins, was all shrouded in the pure white snows, which reflected back up at us like a beacon.

Visibility was now becoming very poor. Returning back to the regular path back up from the rock, we carried on down through the woods, coming on to lower ground still. We climbed down some tricky stone boulder ledges, and then a left turn took us down to the river and some tricky slopes. We passed down an avenue of towering beeches with their large roots intermingling, giving us footage. These beeches here are very old, with their silver grey trunks the size of Roman pillars, and their roots have grown over and under every rock and boulder in their way.

Finally coming to the bottom path by the river, I was looking back up to this avenue of trees when my ears heard and felt a frozen wind pass through from the top path. I lifted my face and received its chill. The chilled wind brushed by my face, and through my hair kissed me with scent. What bliss.

No person had we met yet, but now a lone runner came towards us on the bottom path, saying that he was arranging an organised run in the forest on the Saturday coming, and he did not know if he could keep these arrangements because of the weather. The conversation was brief as he jogged by, and we parted our ways. This was the only person we had seen for all the day, about five hours.

Out of the woods we walked, into an expanse of blinding white. The white wilderness went on forever. It was all so bright I was getting blinded, and started to get a headache.

The canopy of the forest had given us a mellow light, and now the expanse of the sky threw light back up from the snow at us.

We could not resist running about this expanse of snow and began to play like children, throwing snowballs at each other. With our sticks we wrote our love for each other in untouched snow, like the teenagers we once were, and still are inside. This was the first place Charlie had brought me, on his FS1E 50cc Yamaha moped, when we first met in 1975.

As we tramped through the deep snows, we came to Biblins Bridge. I took photographs of the bridge, and the sight got me very excited as every part of the bridge wires was touched perfectly in snow. It was very difficult to climb the flat slope up to the top of the bridge, and I had to get on my knees to take a couple of shots without slipping back down to the bottom. I then told Charlie to run amok on the bridge, to shake all the snow off, so he got on to the bridge and rolled a massive snow ball from end to end like a little boy. I could see the glee in his face, and could hear his laughter with all the fun he was having that echoed the valley this day.

After all the fun, we stopped at a nearby ranger's hut and stood on the balcony for a bite to eat looking out on to the river. A flask of good hot tea with cheese and onion sandwiches made a welcome break, as we had been walking for hours now. A few crows were eyeballing us in the trees, the first birds we had seen all day. We threw them our bits of crust and they were most grateful crows, specially today. Charlie always keeps a pocket full of seeds and leaves them on gateposts for hungry little birds, all over the forest.

The light was now fading fast and it was 4 pm; we were lucky it had stayed light this long. The cold was beginning to bite and we had to walk back up the hill to the car at Doward. There was not enough time or light, and I so wanted to take more pictures. My last shot of the day was a water fountain seeping out of a rock face, frozen solid in time.

It was a slow hard walk up to the car, deep to the knees, crisp and even, (two steps forward, six back) and the air was still and all so silent. I began my calls to the screech owls, which l have perfected over the years with success. I can con them into thinking I am another owl on their territory, and these owls come and investigate. But nothing today.

A fir tree at the side of the path was heavily laden with snow, and l could not resist standing underneath it and pulling at its wispy needles. It gave me a shock when the snow fell on me, burying me and making me feel like a child again. I just could not believe we had this beautiful forest all to ourselves.

Just as we thought things could not get any better, in the distance we saw the gentle deer of the forest foraging. Two smaller deer were feeding while a larger animal kept lookout. Their warm breath dispersed in the cold misty air as we kept still for a few seconds, then suddenly there was eye contact between us and the stag. They all took a turn quickly upon their hooves and bolted away, vanishing within mists and deep forest.

Forest trees slumbered with winter,
Echo silence in flurries deep
Untouched, laden, sparkling even
With my mind's eye, I can now keep

Woodland deers' warm breath disperses
In the distant heavy air,
Locked on sights, their nervous feeding
Spooks a charge, without a care.

THE FOLLY

APRIL 2009

Travelling from Tewkesbury on the M50 at 5.30 in the morning, there was hardly any traffic for miles. It seemed as if we had the whole motorway to ourselves. Ravens and crows looked rudely disturbed at the appearance of our truck in their sights as they fed on dead creatures that had been killed the night before. Streams and waterlogged fields and ditches below the motorway were rising with heavy mists which drifted up and across the road we were travelling. The ghostly white mists merged together from each side of the road, added to this absence of motorway movement.

Turning left at Goodrich, along the lane to the disused quarry, we pulled in for the day. The air was fresh with the scents of wild flowers, and the songs of early birds were many and deafening. One gentleman pulled up beside our truck, the only person we had seen that morning. He seemed to be in a hurry, with all his equipment, as we followed after him up the steep lane called the Folly. Leading to the woods at the top, the moist ground was delightfully married with pale yellow primroses, which balanced the droplets of morning dew upon their petals.

The view from here is magnificent, as Kerne Bridge stands out from the mists that rise up from the river. The bridge in the distance shows off its wonderfully-engineered arches. Coming to the wooded canopy of trees, woodland primroses grow between each step, happy to be just out of the way where people's feet have not trod. I thought to myself that the way plants survive is amazing, and how nature does have a way with her garden, that somehow we could not achieve. Further on and breathless up into the deeper parties of secluded woods, we both at last got to the top out of the darkened woodland now left behind. The sun was coming up slowly and spectacular views across the valley lay before us, in all their newness and early morning glory.

There is a point here on the hill which is called the Trig, once used for Ordnance Survey map making. It made a very good tripod to put my camera on to photograph a few breath-taking pictures. A thick clouded mist hovered above the river, masking the river's flow to the tide, while Goodrich Castle in the distance, a tired ruin, stood alone upon this vast landscape. The castle looked full of centuries as the river curved around the ruins, caressing and swathing them in a veil of white mist.

As we walked along the top of Coppit Hill and followed its regular path, clumps of delicate blueish mauve dog violets and soft dewy primroses had bedded themselves about the thick, rich tufty grass, all wet with fresh dew. Young ferns were yet to appear, and the bright yellow prickly gorse added brightly to this backdrop of riches. From afar looking down into the distance my gaze was distracted and disturbed by an unfortunate sight. I had to look closer, even though Charlie told me to come away. The body of a poor badger lay motionless and stiff on its back, lying just outside the hole to its sett. The body was in good condition, a young adult, and its teeth were revealed in an expression of pain. Its fur coat was perfect in colour and not bloodied at all, but there was a visible injury to its back leg and a bone was sticking out white from the leg muscle. Something told me this had not long happened, possibly in the night.

The surround to the badger's sett looked beautifully decorated by all the wild flowers that grew around the den entrance. In what should have been a peaceful and safe family abode for these animals, it now became apparent that a wretched and cruel deed had been carried out here by man and dogs. The strife this poor animal suffered in such a lovely place made my heart weep, and a tear did fall from me for him that day.

Keeping to the path, not far from Rocklands Wood, the steep banks down to the river are laden with scrub and fine yellow gorse. I recognised within the scrub a narrow deer path leading down into the depths below. I was curious and followed on down through the gorse bushes, taking careful steps to be silent as I went and trying not to crackle sticks.

I did feel very alone, as I had walked on away from Charlie.

Just as I was wondering whether to go deeper, a rabbit jumped out of the shrubbery in front of me, making me squeal. All I could see was its little white bum flick high in the air with its legs in tow as it scurried away from me. Casting my eyes back to where I was going, to my surprise I was greeted with the faces of three sweet little deer peering at me through the gorse. The look on these little faces said it all - "What's that?" They did look startled, but after we had exchanged glances, much to my delight, they took away on their little hooves to their well-used winding paths ever deeper below.

Feeling nicely satisfied that my curiosity had paid off, I made my way back up to the regular path, where many blackthorns arched and overhung the pathway with full blooms as soft and white as snow flurries. The bees are early risers and their little fine wings buzzed merrily about the frilly blossoms of this blackthorn. As the bees danced upon these lacy blooms, tiny petals fell, to litter the ground like confetti while the hum of hundreds of beating wings filled the stillness of the early morning.

★ ★ ★ ★ ★

Deeper down alongside Rocklands Wood, old and mossy stone walling had collapsed and heaped together. This went hand in hand with the messy uncoppiced woodland around about, a sure sign of our times, displaying the fact that our way of life and living needs have changed. But to our eyes the beauties of the woods were ever present. I found a lesser purple orchid - there were quite a few here, growing by tree stumps. I was delighted to be able to take a macro shot of the orchids, which were beautiful in colour and appearance. One would have expected the plant to have a delightful scent, but upon a sniff test, where I had to get on my knees to ground level, I found they had no scent upon them at all. The description in my book of super scents would have the orchid's aroma to be like cat's pee.

Descending our last rocky steps to the bottom of Coppit Hill, we climb over the gate into the field, where many sheep with their offspring are grazing. The lambs chase each other through the field as the moms keep an eye out and continue to feed on the grass. The echoes of their presence fill the valley as we tread through the stinky sheep cobbles.

Down on the banks of the Wye, we watch the river carry on its course. Charlie gets his hip flask out and we share a neat nip of whisky at eight in the morning. The spring sunshine gives us warmth, and we sit to eat our sandwiches with a flask of tea. Some people up on Yat Rock are also out early and are peering down at us, so we give them a wave and they wave back.

We continue to walk left along the river into the woods, and down the path past the memorial. Further on from here I decide to jump a gate into the wood which did not seem to go anywhere, though once it must have done. Within this overgrown area I discovered an old abandoned boat. There were holes in its metal bulk and the hull was completely full of soil, with a tree growing in the middle of it. Near by was coiled up pulling gear, left where it was last abandoned, never to be used again. Maybe this boat was used at some time in the last century for crossing the river with people and goods.

Morning mists on Folly's Rise,
Emerging high the moving tide
Laid bear the ruins swathed in white,
The land is fair, with all disguise.

Diamonds are dew, on primrose yellow,
Violets are blue, with bird song a-bellow,
Badger is dead, they took his life,
Lies stiff in the grass, fought wretched with strife.

Secret paths twine down bright gorse,
Little faces connect with my mind
Moment of silence, we are but one
They speed away on tracks ever deeper,
Upon slopes, they take the good course
My heart remembers our misty meeting,
When silent we four souls were greeting.

A reluctant clamber up back to my world
The craggy path is embroidered with snow
Arches, busy wings, in the early morn
Secludes darkness down by Rocklands Wood
Glancing farewells behind lacy blackthorn.

And ancient stones moan their divide,
Tumbling helpless like sprawling hags
Down to the fields of fertile land
Harkens cries to babes at water's edge,
On the banks of the river Wye.

THE PRIMROSE PATH

≈

SPRING 2009

The old railway bridge across the Wye at Lydbrook is just about passable if you want to walk across to the other side of the river. There are big gaping holes in the boards now that reveal the river below. All manner of shrubbery, including small hazels and birch trees are established, taking up residence in the empty bolt holes which held the rails on to the sleepers.

At the end of this bridge the other side of the river is Welsh Bicknor. From the bridge to the left path by the side of Park Wood is a building of significant interest, which may be part of the history of Courtfield Estate. The house is now a hollow shell with overgrown trees which have invaded the windows and doorways. It looks very grand, with complete fireplaces in the upstairs and downstairs rooms. The outside windows are made of large carved pieces of stone, and on the main doorway facing the river the outer stonework has been worked to a bevel edge.

The building has no roof, because many of the roof tiles are on the ground, partly buried in shrubbery, as time here has had its way. Most of the roof tiles have fallen into the building. Outside at the back is a pretty enclosed garden; you can just make out a boundary built up around the house by stone wallings. The stones are large and carefully chosen to size to make a good wall. They are worked well in together and covered in green moss.

There are animal stalls outside by the garden, sectioned individually, maybe for pigs. Each has a pen of four or five sections and a narrow walkway to lead the animals in and out of the stalls. This area is at a lower level than the house. I do not think that time has sunk it, as it made sense to keep the animals at a lower level than the living quarters.

A cellar is just visible, with a metal grid twisted inside the house floor, because at the front of the house facing the river is a hole covered by a flimsy board. Beyond this hole is revealed a drop down to the river and muddy bank. I'm sure the river would have flooded this cellar many times, so it is not clear why it is here.

Alongside the river away from this building, the pathway is littered with fallen trees. We all had to climb under and over them, as people do not walk here very much, and it has been a long time since someone has tried. It is easy to understand how old tracks and paths once walked by man and beast can be lost with time as nature takes over, as it always will.

Through the bracken up into the shady parts of Park Woods, we keep to the regular path. Ladies' smock amid the bracken stands tall and pinky mauve, its perfect little heads bunched together, and tiny shafts of sunlight stream down through the trees, bringing a dappled effect to their quivering pinky petals.

Scattered all over the wood are wild primroses. I did find some which that had grown into a perfectly round ball shape. Hover flies and little bees dance about their creamy-yellow spring blooms, with their scents delicately sweet. This pathway eventually ends at a stile, and beyond lies a rich green field, beautifully edged with purple wild dog violets.

In these fields by the side of Park Wood, and out on to a land called the Green grows ageless blackthorn sprinkled about the landscape. Two gnarled old pear trees on the slopes are laden with snow-white blossoms. The land here has a slight incline, and is quite wet underfoot as you walk up to the constant trickle of a spring that comes out of neighbouring woods. An old stone trough, built into the grassy bank, is full to the brim with the outpourings of these spring waters. The late afternoon sun shines down on the water trough, very small and discreet, and catches glints of yellow sunlight, revealing colours within its contents of mosses and water plants.

Charlie climbs a fence to look into the shrubbery; something has caught his eye, something with an upturned curling shape. Charlie lifts the leaves, and as he pulls the object out and holds it up I see that it is a deer's antler. It looks well weathered and of a good size, and must have been under the leaves for a long time. This was the antler that got away from the deer, as I have been told that when deers' antlers drop, they eat them, as they are a good form of calcium for them. I am most happy to own a nice piece of forest animal, as I can put it up on my oak beam at home. We all look proudly at this antler that once graced a fine stag, equipping him with the weaponry to fight his place in the forest.

Later we retire to a grassy rock at the top of this field to eat our cheese and onion sandwiches and enjoy a good strong flask of tea. Our ears listen blissfully to the cries of livestock in the distance, and we all take in the pure tranquillity of peace and deserved rest. The views from here are clear and stunning with the richness of further forests. But the air quickly becomes cooler, as the sun's warmth fades with the chill of impending early evening.

My mother-in-law Mary, now 80 years young, never seems to flag easily, so marching on with her effortless vigour, we all stride back on up to the folly.

Oh how the spring has again sprung
New buds appear, forth ripe to burst
Swiftly away goes happy at their pace
Past into spring, it's all now begun.

Ladies' smock in bracken and verge
Neighbours with stars called celandine,

129

As in the fields a frenzy of mad dandelion
Turns heads on stalks, sweet cowslip fine.

But this year seems to be a race,
Where bluebells strived to be her first
And April sings for summer heights,
Distanced the memory of winter's worst.

Blackthorns lace-mottled fill the land
And busying nests make early made
Blossoms of cherry, crab and apple
Fair thick their bloom, seems quick to fade.

For now the may returns like snow
Blackbird is proud, in May he sings
Hang heavy her boughs for all to see
Blinding grandeur the hawthorn brings
To the gentle touch of God's sweet hand.

CADORA WOODS, REDBROOK

MAY 2009

It is Redbrook in late morning, and a dry bright day. Looking up from the road we are greeted by the rich jewels of creation, bluebells and wild garlic growing together in the banks and up into the woods. These perfect formations of wild flowers of the season have spilled down out of the woods and blended as nature knows best.

Leaving the car by the old railway bridge, we walk across the Millennium Green, which is managed by volunteers. From the local shop we bear right to climb the 67 steps up into Cadora Woods. The people of this community at Redbrook are very welcoming to visitors, and they talk to us and other people from their gardens, as we all ascend and descend these steps.

The long climb up from the steps brings us to hedgerows up along the lane to the woods, and we are blessed with an abundance of red campion and greater stitchwort. The views from here look over to Redbrook, and on into the distance is the old railway bridge, under which the river twists blissfully through and under and away. Miles of fertile fields by the river and beyond merge together gaily with the backdrops of rich forest land. A most delightful sight from this high point, and a real picture postcard.

Entering Cadora Woods, the warm air changes to a still coolness. The damp earthy aromas mingle with the sweet scents of bluebells and wild garlic. Ancient small- leaved lime pollards stand towering up from the forest floor, and small streams of sunlight peep through their branches, kissing the wild flowers down below. On the pathway through lies a gnarled old mossy tree stump, where wood sorrel and wild honeysuckle have taken up residence, living happily together in its pocket holes.

A second path edges around to the left where lush fields lie. Two young horses in these fields catch sight of us and begin to compete for our attention. They are very frisky and naughty and keep biting each other. Around the field by another gate, a grand old shire horse who shares this same field comes up willingly to this side gate to greet us. He is a sociable animal and is most happy to receive our fuss, having his ears and nose rubbed and gratefully accepting our freshly-picked grass from the other side of the gate.

Continuing our journey up the lane I take macro photographs of what Mom said were yellow blind nettles in a clump. We then find a grassy bank and have our sandwiches and a flask of tea. The grazing land beyond echoes with the sounds of baby lambs in distant fields. Up in the trees above us sings a thrush, entertaining us with many pretty tunes; perhaps he hopes we will leave some crumbs behind, and we do.

Further down the lanes by the fields, then over a gate to a forest of dark pines, stands an old tree, hollow and grown out. It must be ancient, as it is quite enormous, and small saplings are sprouting from the bottom trunk, as if a new generation of this species is trying hard to emerge from its shell. As I take photographs of the tree, I can see right through it to the other side, and I catch in the distance my mother-in-law Mary, amazingly fit at 80, sitting on the gate like a girl, and a girl she will always be to me.

The walk back out from the woods leads us to a steep stony path, where my husband Charlie walks on ahead. It is not long before he hurries back to us to say he has caught sight of an owl fast asleep in a tree above. We all creep quietly up the craggy path to this tree of rest, with my camera at the ready. This night bird is indeed in deep slumber upon a branch, tucked away all snug. It is too dark in this area to take pictures of the owl, and we do not want to rudely awaken him, but he has one eye open, and knows we are looking at him. Our presence and whispering stir his departure. As he swivels his head down towards us, the other eye opens with an offended expression. All I catch sight of is his rear end as he takes to flight with large brown swooping wings, lowly down into the lane and away.

We have been walking for hours now, and our Redbrook ramble is nearing its end. Wild cherry trees arch tall above us to the rugged paths below, and their petals are like confetti upon us, still falling with the gentle breezes. Into deeper parts of the woods where no one walks, we find a rich piece of the wood untouched and growing between young cherries, a Garden of Eden growing happy together.

Early purple orchids, with pockets of wood anemone, lesser celandine, sweet violet, and primroses, and a few lone white bells and pinky bells nestle in between the bluebells. This is a beautiful hidden woodland patch.

Towards the end of the day, we come upon an ancient yew tree. I have to slip down this steep bank on my bum to get in a better position to be able to look up at this gnarled and twisted giant of the woods and to get a better photograph of it, because of its sheer size. Another tree that had once grown by this old yew has fallen to the ground in a heap of sticks. The yew would be hundreds of years old, I'm told. Mary jokes down to me that I was the lady of the woods - the comment is fitting, I'm in the thick of it, among the brackens, upon dangerous slopes with a drop over the edge, on my belly, breaking a possible slide with a young tree between my legs. I just make the best of it while I could and among everything I love - the forest.

HONEY AND CIDER

JUNE 2009

Sunday morning early we arrive at Redbrook, walking on to the viaduct. Under the darkness of the railway bridge I find it amusing to see that someone has written with a spray can the words "Wolfman Jack". How they got up under there to do this beats me. He must have been a fit lad, and darn daring to do it, as from the viaduct there is good drop down to the river below.

On this humid June morning, we visit the Boat Inn for a drink. This is our favourite watering hole in Redbrook, and it never fails to be a welcoming place. The community here seems to welcome strangers in like their own, involving you in their conversations. Redbrook people talk freely among themselves, which has been at times quite entertaining, and produced lots of laughs. Canine companions of many breeds are here, and they wander freely about the place, playing with each other and making friends with anyone's children.

The constant flow of natural spring water in this area comes from the woods and makes its way through rock. The woods here are like a rain forest, and the constant wet moss and many fern species survive beautifully. The forest springs eventually filter through the ground down to the river below. The soothing sounds of the water trickling through, carrying down the fresh earthy scents of the woods, begin to tame the mind into a calming bliss.

At the back of the dining tables, upon the higher ground, sits a ready-made pool. The pool has been naturally formed where the crystal-clear spring water has accumulated from the higher woods. It looks untouched by humans. I do remember one spring seeing a duck on this pool. She was surprised to see us looking and did not like it. We thought the baby ducklings must be lying somewhere close by in the ferns. Perhaps their mother preferred this pool to the temperamental Wye.

We purchased some local Penallt honey from behind the bar, and were soon joined by a elderly gentleman who was counting his pennies out of his purse to have a cider. The landlady told us that this gentleman was the beekeeper who had made the honey we had purchased, and this really impressed me.

We took our drinks out on to the balcony with a packet of cheese and onion crisps and a pickled egg, and munched and supped as we looked out to the river. The water looked very low and the air had become sticky and humid. Suddenly we hear the deep rumble of thunder over the top of us, and then the rain began to come down heavily. As the cool rain hit all surfaces, including the steel viaduct which had been so hot for days, it created a steamy atmosphere, like being in a sauna. The dogs and children delighted in the rain and played madly, running all over the place and getting soaked. With the dogs' barks and squeals of laughter from the children, it was a joy to see all such fun.

One young lad began to swim from the other side of the river to his mates on the other side. I watched from the balcony to see the river all around this boy covered in bubbles as the raindrops hit the surface. After a good downpour the rain subsided and a kingfisher in its coat of electric blue skimmed low across the river, skilfully hunting out the shallows for minnows returning to the silts.

Conversation is plentiful here at the Boat, with lots of laughter and smiles. The warm and welcome rains had brought relief and joy to all. There is a lot to be said for good company, fuelled by good local beers and ciders and many delightful flower wines from Lyme Regis in Dorset.

The elderly gentleman at the bar, who answered to the name of Jim, quietly joined us on the balcony to have a chat. While supping his cider, he made us all laugh with his stories. I was amazed to hear that he was 83, and impressed at his stamina to still be farming. Keeping bees is not easy, but his methods had stood the test of time. He was most successful, and made his own honey. He wore a cheeky, infectious smile. His steely blue eyes made me want to giggle, perhaps because he reminded me of my father-in-law Len, who was always teasing me rotten and had that same look in his eye.

Jim was a sociable man and enjoyed company. He told us all about the bees he kept in the woods. He said how good the production of his honey had been over the years, and told us about the losses of his swarms, and about the modern methods of beekeeping, which he did not think much of at all. He thought the old ways were surely the best, as bees did not like change. Then he gave me a cheeky grin and said "Bees are like women, you have to be gentle with them". That made me giggle, because he was looking at me with that cheeky grin, and I do believe he was flirting. And he got away with it, bless him.

★ ★ ★ ★ ★

Departing the Boat Inn in the early afternoon, we walked up towards Craig Woods. Through fields as old as time, I waded with Charlie waist high in lush grasses and wild flowers on that humid summer afternoon. It could get no better than to do this with the man I love.

We made tracks up to a dark embankment on higher ground. Entering Craig Woods it became a very steep walk and a long one at that, and I had to stop a few times for rest. The air was not cool for long as my lungs grew tight. Along the way up into the woods I took the opportunity to get my tape measure out and measure the girth of a large beech, growing up from the deeper wood below. Its girth was 160 inches at the middle. As we walked at a slow pace, we found that it quickly blended into lower hazel woods, eventually with flatter levels along the way. Taller trees on both sides darkened our pathway, keeping everything damper and wetter. Hoof marks can be seen to the sides of the soft soil banks where deer have been climbing through to reach the upper hazel woods.

There was a point where the trees opened at the top of the woods on to open ground dry from the sun. Here the ground was blessed with many wild flowers between the dry grasses. Those I knew included common centaury, self heal and red campion. Butterflies basked here happily in the warmth and light of the day, while others danced together on the many ferns that grew here. We were grateful for the rest and for a much-needed cup of tea and a light sandwich. We had been walking one and a half hours already.

We took a pew on a large pudding stone. Behind us a wild raspberry bush grew, complete with tiny little fruits, the size of a child's thumbnail. They were red and juicy and sweet though, with a real raspberry taste unknown to most. Also in residence here was a mature wild cherry tree, whose ripe red fruit had dropped from great heights above softly down to the ferns below. Perfect forest fare.

Pwllplythin Wood was our path of choice, leading down into these woods where it was wet underfoot with a sandy soil, turning to a muddy brambled walk. The light was good, and views were clear across to Whitebrook. Along this path leading into Pwllplythin stood large fir trees on both sides of the path. Their massive rugged girths displayed colours of dark bronze red, and splayed wide at their footage. These trees quite dominated their places in the forest.

I noticed by this wayside that many honey bees had gathered and created a giant nest in this fir tree. The nest was exposed by a large split which was working its way up the trunk. The mass of bees were climbing all over each other, with the hum of many beating wings. There must have been hundreds in there, and how far up inside the tree the nest rose I had no idea. We did not stay here for long, only just long enough to take a photograph of the bees.

On the path further on Charlie discovered a piece of honeycomb on the ground, not very far from this nest. I thought perhaps some small animal had tried to steal a sweet meal, then beat a hasty retreat from the bees and dropped it. This little piece of honeycomb was perfect, and the size of my hand. I walked proudly away with it, claiming this treasure of the forest and sniffing its gentle aroma as I went, gathering all the more thoughts about this beautiful land.

Black clouds suddenly began to cast over the blue skies and thunder rumbled in the distance as we walked into the deeper parts of the wood. The gouged-out, irregular path down through these woods was messy and unattractive compared to what we had left behind earlier. Boulders were strewn about the place and forest clearance had left upturned stumps of trees, exposing roots all messy and ripped about, and all this cluttered and darkened our strangely cold walk out of the woods as the black sky and rumbles of thunder rolled on over head.

Once out of Pwllplythin Wood we turned into an old forest path that had not been used for years. Up into the undergrowth we went, through waist-high ferns. This we thought was an intended short-cut through, which was interesting but difficult. Our map led us through to Colonel's Park, where. we found our way out to open road, with a pleasant climb uphill past the grand residence of Argoed. I must say I was glad to be out of that last part of Pwllplythin Wood, as to me it did not feel very nice in there.

We were flagging now at the hours and the distance we had walked so far and so long, and the heat was still on. The thunder earlier did not come to much, thank goodness, and although the sun was out now, silver-lined marshmallow clouds floated about the blue skies above. Rumbles of thunder began again to roll over the landscape, and a welcome wind tussled the trees to and fro. We had the cheek to sit in someone's field along this way, perching on a pile of logs to take a flask of tea and a sandwich. Pretty little dwellings down this lane had stopped in a time warp, and mossy old stone walls divided their boundaries with these lush, green parcels of land. Well-stocked vegetable gardens and old-type flower gardens were many, complimenting the wild flowers that lived in the lane beyond their walls.

A trickling brook flowed gently alongside this lane on the pastureland side and was a constant presence with us as we walked through. One property here had a smallholding and a run which housed a very frisky young grey horse, galloping madly about its field, and neighing loud for attention. From here we carried on down through Lone Lane, with the intention of stopping by at the Boat for a last alcoholic beverage. Mine was a glass of cowslip wine, Charlie's a cider, which was well deserved for this epic seven hours of walking.

It was now beginning to rain, but we were back under the balcony at the Boat, nice and dry. Two canoeists pulled up to the banks, looking tired and bedraggled and a bit soggy. Friendly fellows they were. They had been canoeing all day, and looked in despair at not getting a drink, as they said they had left their wallets in the car, miles away at the other end. A local man kindly beat us to buying them both a drink, and a conversation between us all developed. One of the canoeists delved into his dry bag to get his rolling tobacco out, and with joy retrieved the wallet he thought he had forgotten. He insisted on buying a drink for the man who had stood them drinks, and because his fingers were so wet and cold (the joys of canoeing I know so well), he asked me to roll him his fag, which I did. I was 30 years out of practice, but successfully handed him my masterpiece of bad health. I licked the paper well, and he did not mind one bit.

Upon leaving these merry folk to go back to Tewkesbury, one of the locals had a young boxer dog that jumped at anything that moved to play, and that was me as I moved to get up. The dog jumped up at my perkies, and put a muddy paw stamp on each. I was for sure "Redbrooked" as my pretty summer top never did get rid of that beautiful red stain.

FOXGLOVES BY
THE MILLION

JUNE 2009

From the main road past Whitchurch is a small road that
leads off to Welsh Newton. Through the winding country
lanes, high-sided hedges are woven beautifully with wild
honeysuckle, and birds fly busily between them, carrying
twigs for nest building or repair. Their little beaks are
crammed full of worms and insects to feed hungry babies,
and they seem unperplexed at our presence, propelling
themselves forward into the responsibilities of family life
that nature gives us all. The hub of living is all around in
these narrow maze of lanes, and a few working farms are
here, scattered among the landscape. Outside one farm a
lone sheepdog sits faithfully guarding its territory, then a
friendly rugged farmer appears out from the farm building
with a smile for us, even on a Sunday.

We journey through the secluded lanes, rich with foliage
and wild flowers, looking as if they are from another time
past. Mature hanging trees make the narrow lanes look

dusky, and a few homes along the way are well established and naturally suited to the environment. They are beautifully kept, and are colourful little gems.

We soon arrive at the end of the road at Wulstans Farm, to be met by a lush clover field, with various breeds of animals, goats, sheep and cows grazing happily together. The abounding views across these fields beyond takes your breath away, and you can see the tips of the Malverns in the distance. To our right is a long winding footpath, with fields on both sides; Elderflower is abundant here in the hedgerows. Ferns grow rich among the hedges, and are entwined within the shrubbery. Foxgloves stand over head height at six feet tall as they reach for the sky between the ferns. Cows can be heard over the hedges, munching and tugging at the rich white clover which is thickly abundant in their grazing field. From behind the high hedges, as I walk further down the lane, the noise of the cows chomping sounds quite funny when you cannot see them.

I forge ahead without Mother and Charlie, because the excitement of discovering new territory is thrilling to me. I reach a gate which I sit on like a young girl, breathing in the peace and tranquillity of humming insects in this field full of wild flowers, untouched. Buzzing bumblebees master the light meadow blooms, bending the pretty little flowers as they go. Many other insect species are attracted by this meadow fare, which all looks so beautifully natural. Large mature oak trees in the distance, on the edges of this land, reveal buzzards flying gracefully, swooping down on to their territory.

Now that I have had my fill of nature's delights, I walk the rest of the footpath to discover tiny animal tracks in the rich fern foliage. They lead to a slight inclined bank up and into the thick ferns. The tracks fire my curiosity, but the fear of disappearing off into the wild without the others presses me on through. It is quite a stomp into the depths of bracken and foliage squeezing around and above me. I will admit to being slightly scared on my own, gingerly trying not to fall on my camera.

It was well worth it to reach the gem in the crown. Within this seclusion was another world, unknown and undisturbed and not far from the regular path of civilisation. Awaiting me was a very long avenue of foxgloves, a secret garden of gardens. Between the regiments of bronze towering firs on either side, this avenue of foxgloves was a purple haze, tunnelling on, so far from my gaze, and disappearing to the other side of the woods. Softly did these foxgloves with their heavy blooms sway away with the cool gentle breezes passing through, and their willowy stalks bowed to a curl at their tops, displaying a royal finery of hanging purple bells, all full of busy bees. The echoed hummings of tiny beating wings filled the humid summer air in this most secret and magical part of the woods.

I knew I had to return to the others, but I felt lost in time. I did not want to leave, as it was all so fine. I was entranced by these delightful moments, and as I turned with a last look, I wished they were mine to keep forever. Alas I came to my senses and began my return, fighting my way back through deep ferns, slipping and stepping down out of this enclosure, then jumping down over the footpath, partly flooded from rains before. My mother-in-law Mary waited ahead for my appearance out of the shrubbery, and her face was a picture; she looked slightly alarmed at this quick departure, and nearly collided with an unexpected cyclist riding quickly by. I nearly jumped out of my skin. As I appeared in front of him, the cyclist skidded to a halt with a shocked expression on his face and a huff of disgust. Laughter from mother and me filled the woods on this humid summer's afternoon.

As we entered through by Hazel Wood the warm air turned cool and streaks of sunshine peeked through the trees above, kissing the mossy humps of uneven ground below. Trees here that are of age have succumbed to serving as hosts for holly, or worse, ivy. A few trees here are jewelled up to their heady heights with the delights of wild honeysuckle. The leaves and flowers are bigger than the humble garden types, and the petals are white and yellow with scents that fill the earthy cool air. Multitudes of foxgloves reached up tall and vibrant in the lighter parts of these woods, in thousands, and consumed our presence in this blaze of purple. Many bees hummed busily about their business, popping in and out of the foxgloves' funnel bells, giving each a quiver upon every visit.

Further on, a grazing field slightly to the left, off the

footpath, is richly laid to white and pink clover and buttercups, and looks most inviting. There is a gate to enter into this field, and a barn for animals to shelter in, by a dead tree and a drinking pond. There is other shelter here for cows to shade from the cutting winds or burning sun, as big old trees hang over the stone walling that edges this field. At this point we are on higher ground, as the land runs down to the bottom lower woods. The field is empty and no animals are here today, their earlier presence revealed by cow pats strewn about this fertile land.

Charlie walks on ahead, to return to me with four small pink clovers, which he gives to me with a kiss. (I did so feel for Mother because Charlie's father would have done the same for her, but he is not with us, and Mother looked on with a slightly sad expression.)

From this point standing, the Sister Rocks by Doward can be seen. At other times when we have been on the Sister Rock just up over the river, we can see this barn, and when the cows are grazing here they look like black dots.

As we continue our walk back into Hazel Wood, a fox casually walks towards us along the footpath, his bronze coat glimmering in the full sun streaming through as he unknowingly sniffs the shrubbery nearby. Then he suddenly catches sight of us and gently slips away into the long ferns. Along this path, it was wonderment indeed to discover two very old chestnut trees, their girths enormous, as well as their height. These grand old chestnuts are gnarled and twisted with age, and Charlie poses for a photograph. He looks dwarfed by the massive size of one chestnut.

The woodland here is mainly planted to firs, but there is a confusion of different plant species that hide a building. The flat grey stones to this dwelling are consumed by nettles and surrounded by a plant not native to our land, the dreaded Japanese Knotweed. It is a rampant weed, and should be destroyed. This building is hollow, with two downstairs rooms with fireplaces large enough for two to cook on at one time. Two upstairs rooms have open fire places. Outside is a back door entrance and there is a smaller adjoining building where a bread oven in the wall can be seen. All around this building is deep shrubbery and overgrowth, and a few white rusty, holey tin buckets have been left around.

It must be noted that it was a risk investigating this building, as it was very dangerous and unstable. Although I quickly took some photographs, it would have been my own fault if the building had collapsed.

Further on down the footpath are two beeches, close together and of great size. Between them is a disused pulling trailer, used for logging at one time. The trailer was left between these beeches abandoned, and it almost looks as if these trees were spared, as this way of work came to a halt. We take to having our sandwiches and tea on this trailer under the shade of these beautiful beeches, all ours to enjoy on this late Sunday afternoon.

A couple of yards away lies another old beech, crashed to the ground with its roots upturned, while other smaller beeches nearby display engravings of lovers' names and dates, some going back maybe fifty years or more. The names are now stretched with the trees growth and unreadable, but the dates are just visible. These trees are nowhere near as big as the others mentioned by the logging trailer.

It is getting late, so Charlie comes up with the idea of getting off the beaten track and venturing back home by ourselves into Joint Wood. It is like a jungle, and has an atmosphere to match. The wood has a lower path that has not been trodden for years. There is very thick dense woodland, with high ferns to battle through. It is not much fun conquering the prickly brambles as they trip us up and get our feet tangled, and we have to contend with deep boggy paths. It seems a regrettable decision to go this way, as I am worried for Mother. Charlie suffers constant aggravation with the horse flies as they kept biting him, although he is covered from head to toe in lemon-smelling insect repellent. We are swatting and waving madly with broken-off ferns, but it is a losing battle, and I am sure my 80-year-old mother-in-law is tiring of her son's bright ideas.

At this point we come to the end of the wood, to rest under a large old yew tree. Charlie discovers a very old horseshoe among the fallen dry needles under this yew, which he gives to his mother as a souvenir for her garden (or a peace offering).

Our walk is coming to an end and we can now recognise the wood for the trees. Battling on in our wake we are consumed once again, and more richly, by the sight of uncountable purple foxgloves on both sides of the woods each side of us. There must be millions. This beautiful sight we would have missed if we had not come this way. So we are thankful for the experience; it was worth it by far.

I know we are on the right path home because I recognise the other end of the avenue of foxgloves, where I had stood taking photographs earlier. Delightful wild cherry trees are in our midst, along with the irritating midges and algae-covered, mosquito-infested bogs. It feels like the tropics here. Nevertheless all these forest beauties carry us along and on our way back out to the regular footpath.

Before returning to the car, my bag comes out to collect the abundant elderflowers that grow in the lane for my wine. Charlie is enlisted to snip the flowerheads off, while Mother and I pack them in. Poor Charlie - to top it all, along with the horsefly bites, he is on a sneezing mission and feeling sorry for himself. The pollen from these lovely flowers has aggravated his hay fever. You see Charlie is an expert in leading us up the garden path in more ways than one, and infuriating as it may be, it always turns out to be for the best in the end. Thanks Pinky.

PARSNIP & COMMUNION WINE

JULY 2009

In the pub again - oh dear this place is beginning to become a habit. Strangely enough as I write, that's how it looks, but hey, no excuses as we will be walking the Penallt Way again soon. So Ma and I enter the doors of the Boat Inn and sit down to a good old glass each of parsnip wine before we journey up that hill on foot through the narrow lanes.

Our clear glasses of smooth parsnip wine are fast emptying. The wine tastes like nectar and is smooth to the tongue as we both submit to its warming effects. And of course we are feeling pleasantly merry. The wine seems to have given us some motivation in getting up that lane now.

With giggles at the foot of the steep dark road we have to take, we stupidly decide to take a short cut across a farmer's field. Opening the gate, we enter a field full of cows which are sheltering under trees from the flies and heat. The cattle look so big when you get close to them, and they are really smelly and stinky. The mud by the gate is deep and squidgy as we all try to edge the field for drier land, but we are sinking ever deeper into the cow muck and piddle puddles. It's difficult trying to keep our balance, as the parsnip wine has kicked in and gone to our heads. Very silly, as those nearly empty tummies of ours have no food in them to soak the parsnip wine up.

We are laughing our heads off as Ma wrestles with her two walking sticks, and I am up to my knees in it, pulling away from the suction of the mud and cow pats. The cows have a vacant look on their faces and are not much amused at our antics. Some of them just carry on with nature's call and lift up their tails as they do it "full on" and steamy as well.

This is not working, I say to Ma. It's too hard to pass a short cut back up to the lane. I think the wine has clouded our common sense. It's time now for these townies to make a real quick exit. As we both squelch back, laughing as we go and trying not to fall face down in this stinky affair, Ma reminisces to us of her stories in the times gone by, when she was a girl working hard in fields with cattle in Gloucestershire.

Returning back to the gate, dry and safe but feeling rather silly in mind and body, we look back to the field. In the distance we can see a lady with her dog trying to attempt the same feat, but she gives up and makes haste back up the bank to the lane. As we come through to shut the gate, still laughing, with smelly cow muck past our ankles, boots and gaiters, a man walks by. He looks snootily down his nose at

Ma and me in what seems like disgust. I call up the lane to him giggling, we've only had one glass! But he does not look back. I assume he does not approve of the ladies sampling the local wines.

On continuing our journey up to Penallt, a lady with dogs at the other end of the cow field comes up from the field and on to the road. As we exchange good mornings, I recognise her as the lady in the bookshop at Monmouth, who served us with books yesterday. Charlie and I spent a great deal of time that morning, buying books from her store. One of the books I bought Charlie happened to be about Welsh cattle, *Under The Hill* by John Forester. The book Charlie bought for me was *Penallt Revisited* by V F Kimber. A small world really, I think, but then anything is possible when you come to this part of the world, dear old Redbrook.

Penallt becomes a steep walk up for a while, the natural springs from the woods above pouring out generously along the side of the lane. Many species of ferns grow here, entwined about the silver-grey rocks that lead up to the crossroads. The air eventually becomes cool from the canopy of trees above which makes the lane dark. The earthy scents of forest fare are ever with us all. Natural springs are everywhere you look and they trickle on by along ditches and under and through the lovely little cottages. Separation between these sweet abodes is provided by mossy old stone walling, which looks forever green, as these damp conditions keep mosses of many species clinging green and new

Self-sufficiency is the rule here, with most people

growing vegetables in their gardens. Dry wood is stacked up and sheltered by the cottage's wood stores, and there will never be a shortage of that here. A few chimneys were alight, even in July; maybe some people do still cook on wood-burning ranges. There are chicken houses at the bottoms of some gardens, so eggs are important as ever, and apple orchards are in abundance with the coming harvest. Around these winding lanes we come across beehives in the woods, some collapsed and old but some in use, as bees go in and out of the hives. A thought came to me - perhaps these bees belong to the gentleman beekeeper of Penallt who I spoke to at the Boat Inn in my chapter "Honey and Cider."

Our main reason for coming here was to visit the old church of Penallt at the top of the lane. As we arrive breathless at the top, Ma is coping with this all blissfully. She's so fit for her age, and has better knees than us for sure. There's a four-day advent at the old church, a Flower and Village Festival with "Penallt through the ages" depicted in flowers. It is Sunday 19th July, and we all arrive eventually up from the steep lane towards the church gates. While we know that we have missed the other activities of the day, home-made teas and all, we will make it in time for the church service.

The Bishop of Monmouth is taking the service here today at the Old Church. At the church gates, adorned beautifully with the prettiest of flower posies and ribbons, a warm welcome is given to us strangers in the porch. The verger at the door is a man who looks rather familiar, though dressed in his Sunday best - he is Jim the beekeeper.

The Old Church is full to the brim as we take our seats to enjoy the service, and there is also a confirmation ceremony. There are lots of young families here with small children, as well as older people. It is hard to believe that so many people could squeeze into this tiny church, but they have, and it is well cosy.

The flower displays are made with great skill and adorn every part of the church. Candles burn, giving the church a golden glow. The sermon has such meaning, and the hymns are sung heavenwards with joy. We take our places in line with everyone else to receive the communion wine. What a blissful gathering.

Towards the end everyone shakes hands, and upon our departure we notice Mr Kimber's first publication on the table, which we do not have. On asking the church ladies about this book, they tell us that Mr Kimber is here in person. Charlie buys the book there and then - *Penallt, A Village Miscellany* - and we eagerly seek the author out from the crowds for his signature. Charlie still has the book in his rucksack that he bought yesterday, *Penallt Revisited*, so he is hoping to get that signed by Mr Kimber as well.

We are briefly introduced to Mr Kimber in the church porch, but he is in a bit of a hurry, because he has a lift laid on to catch back down the lane. He is a nice gentleman in a large overcoat with snow-white hair. The Bishop of

Monmouth is waiting to shake his hand, along with others in the porchway, and we are worried that we have hassled Mr Kimber to sign our books. But he gladly signs them and it now reads inside the cover "To Charles and Debbie, V F Kimber". I do very much understand Mr Kimber and his passion for writing about this beautiful place, and it was for us a privilege to meet him.

★ ★ ★ ★ ★

Outside in the graveyard it starts to drizzle, and we all shelter under an ancient yew tree which is gnarled and twisted with age. The rain becomes a heavy shower, all humid and summery, but it does not get through to us, as the great yew tree of Penallt keeps us dry. Looking up at its greatness, my mind thinks, if only this great yew could speak to us it would tell us some good stories of old. According to the locals it is estimated to be 1,700 years old.

The rain drifts away, leaving mists rising up from the woods and graveyard, as the ground around is dry and warm from the summer's heat. I take many photographs of this wonderful yew tree, then take the liberty to have a late dinner in the graveyard under the Great Yew of Penallt of tomatoes, spring onions, bread and a chunk of cheese. Ma says she had never had a picnic in a graveyard before.

The grass is very long here and pale with scorch, and this is where I lose my camera lens protector. Looking for it is like trying to find a needle in a haystack, and I give up.

It is a long walk back, but at least it is all downhill. On the way back we eat wild raspberries picked from a bush, heavily laden alongside in the lane. It has been a full and adventurous day, with meetings with many lovely people of Penallt, including a famous one, and Mr J. Saunders for his lovely honey, the best you will ever taste. God bless 'em all.

LOOKING FOR BIGFOOT

⌒

JULY 2009

This was a perfect morning in every way. The early glow of the sun was just rising, and the air was mild, with earthy scents ascending from the forest's brackens. I was really excited at exploring a wood so early and in silence, except for the occupants of this woodland stirring from their slumbers as time went on.

On the darkened footpath down, well worn flat by boots and wheels, we took a right detour into this woodland towards Coalpit Hill, which is mainly covered by coniferous trees. The path leading down was dark and felt quite cold, and underfoot was boggy, with rising dampness from the forest floor. The tall thin bare tree trunks half way up stood close to each other like a regiment of soldiers, giving a hazy effect from rising mists as the early morning sun peeped through in places.

Walking down steeply through bog and fallen bracken, the forest grasses alongside the path were shoulder high. It all looked magical as the sun shone through their willowy stalks and fluffy heads, now blond from the sun. And the grasses swayed so gracefully upon my passing by that I had to feel their softness in my hands. Within the distances of the woods a strange grunting noise sounded from time to time, which I connected to a deer presence somewhere not far away. Buzzards were roosting in nearby pines, and their busy family commotions pierced the early airs.

Taking further careful steps gingerly out of the forest's canopy, the slippery slope out revealed very large hoof prints in the muddy ground. The prints were of good size and fresh. This deer had not long since walked this way before us. I must admit to feeling a bit anxious that we were intruding on prime territory, as the hoofprints in the mud were not very reassuring. I was excited all the same to meet him.

It is easy to let your imagination run away with you as this time of the year when parents are rearing their young. They will ward you off if they think you are too close, as I know from experience. Once at Coppit Hill within the gorses, we came unexpectedly upon these deer with their young. They looked at us and gave the warning sounds, like a grunting cough, and a shaking down of the head as they did it. So we crept away and out of their presence.

I also remember one year wanting to take a macro photograph of a rare orchid at ground level nearby a rock face area, where I knew there to be a family of peregrine falcons. As I tried to jump a fence to take the shot of the orchid on the ground, the noise of the parent falcons was horrendous, a loud continuous scream like a vixen. I did not entertain taking this photograph in the end, because I was too scared. The parent peregrines made no bones about it and started to swoop towards me. I began to feel hunted, and did not fancy getting myself half scalped. It was all innocent on my part, but I did not foresee how well these birds of prey would protect their young although I was a fair distance away from them. Respect at all times must be exercised in the forests.

Getting back to our walk along to Coalpit Hill, the path halts at a fork. We take a right, where the path lies dry and dusty. Wood clearing operations had been going on here some time before. Lots of trees had been cleared, leaving the ground open to be occupied with stark yellow ragwort rising up toward the backdrop of the remaining coniferous trees, where the buzzards could now be seen flying low.

The air was now becoming humid with the warmth of the impending July sun. As I stood upon this path to admire the ragwort's colour against the hot sun, I began to daydream of the deep yellows, thinking how beautiful this all was.

A few minutes had passed when I thought about the coughing noises I had heard earlier on the way down through the forest. Then strangely, just as my thoughts were on the subject, I heard some soft coughs among the ragwort, very close to me. Suddenly my breath was taken away, and

I froze with amazement, as out of the towering ragwort a few yards in front of me emerged a magnificent beast. First a pair of fine grand brown antlers appeared, followed by a large proud head and a strong fit body of prime male size, standing tall and unperplexed on his legs, up out of the yellow ragwort. This stag had been snoozing amid the bracken, and was buried by the yellow ragwort. He had not expected my presence. When I came into his view he looked confidently at me, but with a steely eye, and seemed to have no fear. He was the boss, and we both knew it.

I could not believe my luck, but there was not a chance that I was going to fiddle to turn the camera on and lift it to my face. No, this moment was too beautiful between woman and beast, and it was mine to keep all my life. We just looked at each other for long moments that felt like forever. My emotions were locked until he lightly pranced away from my presence, but he stopped to take a second look at me, and in my stillness I felt like a queen. Then he turned away and lightly went on over the great plains of yellow and into the darkness of the cool pine woods.

Further on away from this path I was upon, a good harem of does could be seen resting in the thickets and grasses with their young, and I knew this was my stag's family. "Bigfoot" that is what I call him. And me, I am just, the lady of the woods.

Boss Who

Boggy sink the pine needles
Intermingle earth's purified rain

162

Where pines stand regimented and dark,
Filling up his mark, dominating territory
Distances far between us blankets
A knitted bracken, near coughs a bark
Then forks a path, ends a question.

Here dust with compact and stones
Man's order ravished through
Ditches leak human rubbish
Buried by nature like bones.

She stands invisible with nature in part
To the stark yellows, blinding with sunrise
While the fawny wings swoop,
Mastering the giants, all in troops
Shrieks to my presence, and surprise.

Breaking the picture, risen from slumbers
Unperplexed, confident, no fears,
The Dominant Beast his crown firmly fixed,
Turned his jewelled brow with a steely eye
Held my love for him, locked away my tears.

Who has the upper hand?
Our minds meet and communicate
No technology, no higher animal,
Greets respect between us, to honour
The same soil, the same land.

Later:

Amidst chaos of the upturned

Rises the royals of "the royal"
Lords and ladies, July returns
Red shiny berries sweet
Hide with me through blond grasses
Peeking into withery nests, warm with his babes.

A WONDERLAND
OF MIRRORS

JANUARY 2010

Night is passing, and the early hours of a new day are slowly emerging. All is to be magically revealed with the secret beauty that forests give. When you are the first to be there and the first to imprint the new snow, the day is yours.

Everything is asleep, and only the silence and a stinging wind tell us that the forest is frozen from the deep snowfalls of the night before. A surface of white sparkles is frozen like an iced cake. A severe frost has passed through, and the coming sun is waking out of the blue skies.

Such a depth of snowfall I had not seen since I was a child back in the sixties. The texture was different from previous snowfalls; it was light and fluffy, and effortless to walk through. Heavy laden was the snow, gently placed on tiny twigs and tree trunks where the winds had stuck the falls against the tall tree trunks, vertical or horizontal. The drifts had hunted out the skeletons of the forest, and there the snow had stayed packed tight, balanced perfectly, with the help of Jack Frost. In Doward and Lords Wood the woods are now wearing another costume, one of her finest.

Upon the landscape the snow's surface lies undisturbed, resembling an iced cake lightly sprinkled with lustre dust. As we go on through the woods, the snow sparkles and twinkles delightfully in the low midday sun.

A lone figure sits high up on the pinnacle of a tree, motionless within his territory; a bird of prey. He sits gathering the warmth to his body from the highest point and the low sun strikes his plumage proud as he sits wonderfully ambered. His graceful form stands out against the blue, and no call sounds from him. This wonderland is another world, and silence reigns, for not a voice or a wing can be heard; there is no noise except our own heartbeats.

We continue on to the familiar path, now invisible, and yew trees stand in our way like a picture postcard Christmas, heavy laden with soft needles. We are both forever hopeful of more surprises as we make our way towards the Sister Rock. This high point feels to us on top of the world. Every lump and bump and curve of the rock face is drowned in deep, perfect, untouched snow. The rock face presents a daring sight, and where is the edge to the drop below? Snow blobs over the edge of the rock, frozen. Jagged mirrors of frost line up in regimental form, all the same in shape and size, reflected perfect against the sun, a mass of sparkles.

To the right, the view is up the Wye towards Monmouth, and over the A40 a cattle barn stands alone in the wide corner field where the sun shines on it whatever the season. This is the field I wrote about in my story 'Foxgloves by the million'. This field and the Sister Rocks connect faces from here on both sides, and today it is a picture postcard.

The landscape is incredible, as the detail of its shape is now more prominent. The sun is bright and warm, but it does not melt away these new moments in time. For the few hours we spend here we lay a thin plastic sheet on the rock ground to sit on. We both enjoy a cup of tea and a left-over box of Christmas mince pies. We are on the top of our little white world and with the best views ever. As the hours pass, and just before the fiery sun begins to lose its warmth, disappearing slowly behind the forest trees, a stream of sunlight beams a special place for us left from the day. Charlie and I embrace the embers of this day as we connect as one, and do naturally what all forms of life do.

Upon our departure the teenage girl in me returns and I write our names within a heart, pierced with a Cupid's arrow. Looking back on love, I return to the path a mature woman.

Upon the naked forest,
She keeps her eyes closed tight
The hollow chill passes through,
Within her flesh and sticks
He has come to her in the night.

Awaken not, to the heavy fall
Their dormant state, that is true
His scent is swift upon the wind
She fondly submits, to let him in
And answers to his coming call.

Under canopy universe drapes silence,
And drowns deep his heavy load,
Her costume parades proudly new,
Vertical or horizontal, sparkled hold,
Upon a story to you are told.

Appearances of weight, but weightless,
Thrown from the heavens made
Within creation its science,
In flight, upturned upon a dove's wings,
God crafts the land, in all his greatness.

Within a rock, down by rivers,
My love, my love, you and I are,
Those wonderland in mirrors.

The forest waits for her love, and he comes surely to her as a
lover, and leaves his cover.

THE RIVERS RUN RED

FEBRUARY 2010

The skies are drenched with darkness, and thunder rumbles in defiance overhead. The filthy clouds begin casting all their water at you. The earth below is choking helplessly at the unmerciful downpour. It hits the high grounds hard and they saturate as it penetrates the soils of Herefordshire. Brick-red waters flow vigorously out of the fields and lanes and roads and drains, raging through all channels together as one. The meetings of the waters race towards one destination, flowing fast and uninvited into the River Wye.

This day the river really did run red, and was spilling its fill back towards the land. The last snowfalls of January had left their mark on us all, and the melting process was a contribution to this unwelcome splurge of weather that had battered Wales.

Redbrook was our destination as we travelled the wild A40 road. On to Monmouth, the left turn at Troddi Bridge was tricky. The road was waterlogged to the maximum and just passable, with a risk that there would be no way back. The brooks that ran along farmers' fields, passing under the road, threatened travellers with their mad rush to gush back through and over the road. I began to think it was inevitable that we would have to find another way back home, and in the dark.

We pulled into a corner layby until the skies had cleared, but although the heavy rain had stopped, the water continued to rage out of the neighbouring fields and straight across the road, making it almost impassable. The red rushing waters came closer down towards the place where we had parked in this little layby corner. Cars travelling the road towards us still thought nothing of speed as water gushed through the hedges at them. As the cars dashed by, it looked as if they were about to take off, wings of red water flying out from each side. Thunder continued to roll on overhead, with flickers of blinding sheet lightning.

We had waited for some time in this corner layby when my son Charlie phoned me up back in Tewkesbury, to ask how to make tuna fish cakes. While discussing the humble culinary delights of fish cakes with my son, I told him how I had made them. In the background I could here my grandson Callum tugging at his father's apron strings for attention, or impatience to have his tea. Apparently all was calm on the Tewkesbury front for a change (it is such a watery old place). But here in Wales was just how I liked it, and with a sure premonition that something good was going to happen to write about. I thought, Redbrook here we come, my faithful friend, she never lets me down.

As Charlie tried to travel sensibly up that watery old road, I looked to my right towards a derelict cottage which was set back from the road. Upon the collapsed gable end of the cottage sat a miserable, wet through, bedraggled buzzard. His colours could just be seen, and his wings had fully caped his body.

We took the B4293 to a sharp turn up a small road, then a sharp left to a small lane up by Cae Caws House. On the land of Church Hill Common, in places of exposed land, large blobs of snow lay unfrozen and solid still from the last snowfalls. A hen pheasant sat on the old stone walls staring at us as we passed her by, to the winding lanes of Penallt Church. Old and disused farming objects lay strewn in the thickets of land beyond these stone walls.

Up in the woods a complete red tractor from the 1940s had been left rusting away. I could only think it had been used for shifting forest wood about instead of the horses.

And then we were both met with a frustrating sight. The lane was blocked by a car which had tried to get through the red waters, which were nearly half up to its doors. The car was clearly immobile, and waterlogged and was going nowhere. Steam filled the lane from the heat of the engine, and the poor lady driver looked petrified.

A Welshman with his trousers rolled up to his knees, exposing his white bloodless legs, was trying to push the car forward, but to no avail. Meanwhile a man with an Irish accent stood on the now flowing grass verge, also with his trouser legs rolled up, helplessly supervising all the frustrations. Now along came Charlie the Englishman to offer his help; we had a chance with our Trooper 4 x 4, and we did have some canoe straps in the truck, which was well strong enough for pulling. I think we were these unfortunate people's saving grace, and how glad they were to see us at the other end of the lane.

The Welshman had been in the water trying to help for some time, and he shook with the sheer cold that was now getting to him. He showed us his numb and bloodless legs and feet. He and Charlie coupled up the tow hook to the car, and the Irishman laughed as he came up to us, saying "What's the chance of a Welshman, an Irishman and an Englishman being in a situation like this!" It was rather funny, but we saved the day for these people. We reversed back from where we had come to pull their car out of its dilemma. Good job we had a big car with the engine power to pull, as it was a hard slog to get this car out of the rising waters.

Well that was our good deed for the day, and the look on their faces when we arrived was amazing, a surprise for us all in more ways than one. We nearly did not take that turning, as we were going to drop in at the Boat Inn the other way. But then we changed our minds and reversed back up the road to turn in towards the Old Church Penallt. "Surely true God is Good." Now I had something to write about all right.

We were about to reverse and carry on with the journey

back home, but as we looked out of the car window down towards our wheels the lane was so narrow. Every ditch along the lane was turning into a fast-flowing river of brick red water which was mounting the road surface. Little springs from out of the woods were spurting high out of rocks as the waters had risen. A large cottage along this way has at the bottom of its garden a small decorative bridge, which diverts the springs through the garden and under the lane. Today this spring had forced it way through, firing red waters high up into the air; it looked so strange.

We did take a wrong turn for some reason, in all this commotion, into a narrow road that was unrecognisable. It could not be seen on the map, so it had to be a private road. The cottages here were all dark and no one was in. We thought for a moment that we were jammed in this narrow lane. The stones and rock pieces that were holding the wall banks back from the cottages were sodden from all the wet, and had collapsed upon the small road we were on. It took Charlie a six or seven-point turn to get out. How he turned our vehicle around I will never know with a car that big.

We looked back to where we had come, where the end cottage had the whole field to their back garden. The field was not far at all from the River Wye, and it was scary to see how the river was slowly creeping up over the banks and into the field. I'm so glad we did not get stuck down there.

As we were passing away from the fields, looking grey and unfit for any animal to upon graze upon, the gormless-looking sheep were wet through, their sodden fleeces weighing heavy on them. Darkness came quickly. As we turned out from the B4293 the flashing lights of a police car blocked our passage out, and we hoped it was not an accident; the road was badly flooded, as I thought it would be.

THE DAY THE SKY STOOD STILL

~

Did you ever wonder why we do not get summers like we used to? It has a lot to do with air traffic, and all the pollution aircraft leave behind in the atmosphere. The summers I remember when I was a child in the 1960s were hot and dry, just as summers should have been. It seemed that our six-week summer holidays from school went on forever, and every day was sunny. There was hardly a day when it rained, except for night times when thunder and lightning appeared after the build up of all those hot summer days.

The eruption in Iceland in April 2010 threw a lot of volcanic ash into the atmosphere, and all flights were cancelled until further notice because it was too dangerous to fly. For a short time the skies were clear of noise and pollution and the sun shone beautifully out of the blue. We had all the rays to ourselves, and oh what bliss it was! A time never to forget, and a time we may never see again, at least in my lifetime. As long as I have been alive there have been aeroplanes in our world, but to experience a week of the way things had once been when there was no such thing as air traffic was wonderful. Life was so different, in a way I could have never imagined it.

In the forest all life is contained, and ready to unravel and reveal her new beginnings. When all the sights and sounds of springtime begin, the ash from that volcano could not have come at a better time of the year. We were at one with nature in more ways than one, because this was how it used to be a long time ago. Forget the workings of mines and quarries and smelters and limekilns and all the workings of man, with all that noise and pollution - that must have been worse than air traffic and motorways put together. It was a time of the humble handsaw which man used to fell his wood and live in the forest, keeping himself and his family warm, and cooking his hunted animals. The only movements then were of animals moving around these rich forests, such as the bear and wolf, and others that have long disappeared.

The century I now live in has given me an insight into that time, for a week, and as we walk the glades of Doward towards the Sister Rock, you could hear a pin drop. The silence in the forest made your ears hum, as you hear the blood moving within yourself. The birds of springtime became an orchestra, and the only sounds dominating the skies were buzzards cruising the blue, their calls of the mating season piercing the silent air. I am now looking up

176

to count fourteen buzzards coming together with their calls, diving at each other, and playing the courting game.

A rustling in the crispy leaves that have fallen upon the forest floor catch my ear and I look up to see a prancing fox, beautiful and bronze, large in size, with a tail that sweeps out from its body majestic. The fox stops in its tracks and stands with a slightly raised paw, looking my way, examining me for a few seconds, then disregarding my image as if I were a tree. The fox makes its way from the regular path, through the gladed beeches, up the bank and down into the old grey quarry. When the snows fell heavy here one year, there were paw marks across the fresh snow that sparkled like tinkling glass, on the same route across the quarry to where the fox went today.

I do remember blackberry picking one year here, down by the quarry gate where the spongy moss glows a strange fluorescent green, almost yellow. It was not far from here that I began to harvest those sweet berries in my sandwich box. As I became engrossed with trying to reach the fattest, ripest berries, I paid the price of pricking myself, getting caught up and tangled in thorns and brambles and putting my hands on big creepy September spiders which ran from my clumsy fingers.

My foot had trodden on something soft. Looking down at my feet to see what it was, I squealed at the sight of a very large dead fox under the brambles. I threw my blackberry fare up into the air, and edged away from the poor animal.

Afterwards I could not stop looking at the fox, and wondered why such a healthy-looking animal, in such good condition should be sprawled out here. There was no injury, and he looked so perfect. I thought that if the fox had been poisoned, he would not be in such a relaxed position. He was not old and tatty, so it did not seem that his day had come; a bit strange.

★ ★ ★ ★ ★

Getting back to the day the sky stood still, with one day in the forest out of a week for me, my route on the path down to the rock had residents, a large ants' nest. It has been here for the four years I have been coming to Doward, so it could have been a permanent fixture here long before I came. Over the years we have watched the nest grow wide and tall, as the wood ants gather pine needles from neighbouring pine trees. On looking into the forest ants' little world, you can clearly see them carrying eggs and transporting them around deep down into the nest.

Ants are very intelligent, and have a pull-together system that works for their survival. These forest ants are bigger than garden ants and will stand up on their back legs to anyone, perhaps when they feel threatened. Their bite nips a bit as well, so don't fall on a nest, because you won't want them marching around in your trousers.

Watching the forest ants today I have noticed a disruption

within this nest, and what a shame because it seems some bird has found and disturbed their home. All the top has been dug out deep and tossed about. Oh dear! all that hard work, and with a fair few of their numbers noshed by a bird, but that's nature of course. There are still thousands of these ants left to repair the damage, and the noise of their little feet running about madly to fix their home can be heard sharply in the silence of the forest. All those little bodies scrabbling over each other and the nest debris sounds like someone crackling a thin plastic bag by your ear.

I wished I could help them in their plight, but knowing that nature must take its course, I had to remember that insects are just like us, having a choice about what home improvements we make. So I think my attempts to help them cover up may not have been appreciated.

I know of many locations now around the Forest of Dean where there are these forest ants nests, some of them most impressive. During the winter months they nests are camouflaged by the fall of the autumn leaves, and in winter the ants are still resident deep down, though all will be quiet on the home front. I do know the ants shut up shop early in the year, and people passing by throughout the winter months would not even know they were there.

Getting back to this day upon the Sister Rock, it is a kind one, and the sky seems to go on forever, wide and high to the heavens. True blue is her colour, and as the fiery sun sits glowing warm, it is unrestricted by blundering clouds and may share its warm rays upon us for April. We sit down at the rocks' edge, lie upon the warm limestone rock and stare up into an undisturbed world that we never knew before. I could have died here happy today, and evaporated into the elements, as peace overwhelmed me. Buzzards caught the sunlight in the blue as they softly soared in circles above us, with their gentle cries to the freedom of the sky.

LITTLE DOWARD REVISITED

~

It had been a beautiful spring and summer so far, with tropical conditions and an unfamiliar atmosphere. It had to rain some time, but it was so long coming. The feeble attempts at rain lately wouldn't wet a gnat in this heat. Although wet summers can be a pain, when we wait so long for it to be a good summer it gets scary.

Conditions like these take me back to the summer of 1976. The soils were already parched and cracking open. But you never want this weather to stop, as it is so heavenly to wake every morning and pull the curtains open on the brightness of the summer day.

I awoke from my sticky, restless slumber to the fresh morning and peeked through the curtains to see that the fiery sun had risen before me, indicating that once again it was not going to be lenient with the heat.

My Freelander was due for an MoT service at Crocker's Ash that morning, and I had to travel from Tewkesbury early, regardless of the fact that it might take the whole day to do the service. The mechanic said it would get done somewhere along the line in the day. The mechanics were on overload, so we took the slot.

So we were carless and left to our own devices. Charlie and I walked along the dry dusty roads to Doward through the lanes, where life seemed so slow and old. The heat was rising already from the little road, and the sun bore down hard upon us out of a true blue sky. There was not a cloud in sight for relief. Horses in the lush surrounding fields were feeding greedily on the rich grasses and swishing their tails to keep the biting flies off them, while other horses in neighbouring fields were basking within the overhang of the trees in the cool corners.

The narrow lane up to Doward Woods was a real knee-jerker. I never felt it so steep. In a car the gears do all the work, but just you try walking it. Charlie and I had to keep stopping for breath, and it was damned hard.

The shade from the horse chestnut trees that towered above the lane offered a little coolness. Sadly their rusty, shrivelled leaves looked as if they had had a premature attack of autumn. But autumn does not look like this; these trees have succumbed to a disease. I just hope it does not carry on in future years and lead to their destruction.

The elderflower bushes that grow abundantly here behind the hedgerows have little lacy umbrella heads which release sweet creamy scents that fill the humid airs. Buried within the fresh grasses along the lane beneath our feet are the prettiest wild flowers. These little gems of summertime peek out in bright yellows, pinks, blues and purples. Even the field bindweed looked delightful and delicate as its pink and white funnels crept along the verges.

Within the woods at Little Doward we stopped for lunch, sitting on a forest seat which has been dedicated to the memory of someone. This place is familiar to me, as I wrote about it in my diary for 2008. This is the home of my "Giants of Silver" and these skeletal beeches can still be seen from the top of this site. Looking down upon them, they no longer look silver; their dead weathered appearance has become dreary grey. Their starkness is not suited to the summer light, and the forest is ready to consume their dead forms.

We continue to walk up the worn-out track, stony and steep from the earth upturned by the big wheels during past woodland clearance operations. But nature is quickly taking over. In 2008 I stumbled upon this land on a very windy day, and rain was on its way towards us. The landscape that greeted me here gave me a shock, as the landscape looked raped of its soul. It was a scene of ruthless devastation. I don't know how else I expected woodland clearing to be carried out, but I found it sickening. It seemed the guts had been ripped out of this area. I have written about this in the chapter *No Man's Land*.

But I have taken recent photographs of this place, and I can only say that nature is king. My heart sang to the joys of what looked like a Garden of Eden. Man could never create such a garden. He can make the mess, but I can only say that heaven's seeds will proclaim all that is dead and make it new, as it is today.

Walking up through this turfed-up land we found six-foot-high thistles growing abundantly. There was a constant busy hum of many bees and flitsy flies, hovering and dancing upon these towers of thistle blooms. Great mullein is a dominant flower here; they stand tall and snake-like, with soft furry silver rods (hence the alternative name Aaron's Rod) which are rich with yellow blooms to the tips, with a curl. They burst forth out of a large spray of soft silver leaves.

Upon our further travels we came across a gnarled and twisted veteran beech, growing at a angle. The tree had a silver badge fixed to the trunk, so it must have been very old and protected. Looking back over this land at Little Doward before we disappeared down into the shade of the woods, my gaze returned a picture into this world, ablaze with sweet summer colour, of a distant memory of what had once looked so torn apart, and had now returned tenfold: a Garden of Eden.

We had now walked through the woodlands and lanes of Little and Great Doward for eight hours, and the time walking this familiar and unfamiliar territory had flown by. I peeked over hedges at Great Doward, where fields were golden in the sweltering afternoon sun. The harvested fields that sloped down, meeting the wood's edge, displayed patterns in new bales of grass. Buzzards swooped confidently feet above the field, with their spanned wings skilfully maintaining their flight as they scanned the stubble low and slow for rabbits or carrion.

The road was long and hard underfoot, and exhaustion was beginning to set in. All day we had seen no one at all, except for a young man who came striding up towards us. His hair was in rasta style and he wore rolled-up trousers and hobnail boots and carried a bag on his back. His clothes were rough, and he looked as if he had been taking advantage of the summer sun for months on end. I thought perhaps he was sleeping out of doors, as he looked like a new age traveller, a young drifter. He had a rough carefree dog with him running on ahead, with a scarf round its neck. When we were children these people were known to us as hobos or tramps, and I remember feeling scared of them because of what mother used to say.

We decided to take the scenic views up towards Sandyway Lane, and it was worth it. Here this secluded area little gems of cottages are sprinkled on the hillside. They are beautifully managed in the traditional way, with old varieties of flowers. Some of the gardens have strange ornaments, hand-crafted by the owners. I once found these strange ornamental features in a garden further up into Doward Woods a few years back, when I first discovered this mysterious place. Even now, I was frightened to take photographs of the dark, horrible-looking creatures in one garden. I did feel a bit spooked.

We came to another cottage here by Sandyway Lane, with a blue gate, called Ganarew Cottage. The front entrance to this residence is in the dark and secluded part of the lane, where an overhang of veteran trees grows twisted and gnarled out of the banks along the lane. There are views from this cottage gate, looking high over the countryside to old Ganarew Farm. Within our own family, my husband's grandad, Fred Ferneyhough, worked here on the farm many moons ago when he was young. The ruins can just be seen in the distance from where I stand outside Ganarew Cottage. It seems funny now to encounter a cottage here named after Ganarew, when the name was often talked about in Charlie's family.

BETTY DAW'S WOOD

～

JULY 2010

It is a warm, dry sunny day as we make a turning off to
Newent from the M50. We travel left at the junction, down
along the dusty road to Dymock. The narrow lanes are
beautifully secluded and the sides are almost grown enough
to meet each other amid the rich July growth. Little hedge
birds fly to and fro between the bursting foliage, singing
blissfully, and all alive to the joys of these beautiful summer
days feeding babies and going on with family life.

Along the road we come to an orchard that sells apricots,
so we stop to buy some. Those juicy velvety apricots on a
hot dry afternoon like this are a welcome thought for
quenching our thirst. As I knock on the door no one
answers. All is so quiet, except for the sweet summer songs
of birds. Maybe the farmer is out? I do not think they could
be in the orchards.

Anyway, I stand by the car waiting for Charlie to return
from finding someone. The fields ahead of me are
abounding and fertile as harvest approaches. High in the
blue soars a lone buzzard as I strain my eyes away from the

187

burning sun. I watch the graceful flight of this buzzard, as he plays effortlessly on the thermals above. I look down at my feet as the sun catches the sparkles within the red loamy soils I stand upon.

Basking in the warmth of the sun against the car, I close my eyes, feeling an emotion in my heart from long ago when I was a child. Apricots, sweet apricots - they were my favourite. We had an apricot tree in my father's garden, and I can just remember being lifted up to pick the fruit from this tree. How I wish my father were still here, he was such a good man. Right up until I left home at seventeen, my mother always made me apricot pie as a treat. But then one day the tree became so old that it produced no more apricots. As for today, we left this orchard empty handed, like the old tree in my father's garden.

My aim was to visit Dymock, as I had my reasons to be there. I felt the need to involve myself with a band of poets, the Dymock Poets, who lived here once. I had stumbled upon these gentlemen in a bookshop, and being a poet myself, I felt a closeness and bond with these men of my great grandfather's generation. I was born within the century when they lived, and our passion for this place called Dymock beats a poet's heart for me. These are the people that we were and still are.

The afternoon was heavy and humid as Charlie and I strolled into Betty Daw's Wood holding hands. The blackberries were already bearing fruit alongside the woods, long before most blackberries, which were still in pink flower. Meadowsweet was in full bloom, standing tall and straight, with fluffy ivory flowerheads packed with hoverflies, butterflies and bees, which I viewed closely. These regiments of meadowsweet gave the warm July airs a sweet and creamy aroma, divine to one's senses, and my favourite of the season. Betty Daw's Wood was quite shaded in places, with the dappled sunshine peeking through the young trees. A few oaks were present here, not greatly old at eighty years maybe, but they were ready for the chop, as the markings of red paint streaked down their barks had marked them out for the axe.

The wild cherry trees all over this small wood were abundant and heavy with fruit. Some branches were just reachable to pull down and pick handfuls of tiny red cherries. So sweet were they that we greedily ate the juicy fruits and stored many in our sack for home.

We returned to the car to travel back up the dusty lane, cutting across the motorway bridge. I looked down at the crazy M50, imagining a time when this road could have been a dirt track or a field, or some part of the forest. The silence that must have blessed this land once I shall never know. But I do feel very grateful for the fact that I live in an age when I can own a motor car. It is my only way to be here, with the poets, with the forest, and to visit what I feel is my home of homes.

I discovered the Forest of Dean at the age of sixteen with Charlie, my boyfriend as he was then. I remember sitting on the back of his yellow FS1E Yamaha 50cc, which had a seat which was about as comfortable as a plank. I have never looked back since, because the M50 gets us here.

It was nearing four o'clock and the skies were turning grey and heavy. Thunder in the distance rumbled as we took the journey through part of Dymock Forest and past the daffodil way. Although the day was nearly through, I did not feel fully satisfied, as time was not on our side, and because the day is never long enough and you just cannot do it all. My intention was to return in the spring of 2011, and to one day walk where the Dymock poets had walked, within the bosom of the daffodils. Then I will have an answer to give back to them, poet to poet.

Lunch, or should I say early tea, was yet to be had, but my tummy was still full of those seductive cherries. The cake and quiche I brought had not been eaten, but the wild cherries we had gorged upon earlier in Betty Daw's Wood kept the grubs from biting for a bit.

We made our way on and stopped under a tree by St Mary's Church at Kempley, and as we neared the church gate it began to spot with rain. The warm humid air was stifling. The approach to the church from its gate and path is indeed a gem in the crown of Kempley. It felt strangely as if nothing had changed over the centuries.

After staying for a while, we explored and drank in this

beautiful place. As we entered the church heavy rain came upon the church windows, and I stood in the pulpit looking out at the congregation of yesteryear. You feel the thoughts of past generations down the centuries within this church; all those prayers and sermons of many men of the cloth, the people and their lives within this land.

I took photographs of the old church, thinking of all the folk in the fields labouring in centuries past. The porch was made of wood, which must have been several hundred years old when it was built.

Signing the visitors' book, I later realised that I had written the wrong date; our visit was on 22nd July 2010.

We left the old church to sit in the car outside under a dark yew tree, with a flask of tea, and our cake was finally enjoyed and eaten. Charlie had now fallen asleep, with a full belly and peaceful within the world of Kempley. My window was open, and as I looked towards a field of flax my gaze settled upon the old church roof through the churchyard trees. It looked so fine, and I was soon to be away in another time dreaming. As I took in the quiet of this place, I would swear I could hear the gentle voices of people in the old church's congregation, yet I knew no one was inside. For a few seconds I really did hear people singing, and I shall never forget it.

Betty

Enter through her wooded glades
Off narrow tracks of marshy soils
Falls bounty rich those cherries be
That fell from high, the forest's spoils;
Leads me on my way, a gate of old,
Where on this land, lie stories told.

I gladly rest my arm upon this gate,
Nearby a bough twists holly tree
And beats wings in song to my ears;
And there I think of you, my poets,
Past in time, past by many years.
I now hold the torch you threw to me,
Because in time and place, we poets relate.

Beyond the gate, into a heaven's fields,
Danced the sway of the blondest grasses,
Upon gentle breeze, a thousand miles long,
Up to the hills, a scorched multitude throng.

July brought forth a maid's flowing hair
Bobbing up and down behind the hedge,
The child bounces free within her youth,
To a horse's prance, upon a fine young mare.

Then returns a call, my love into the wood,
Joined hands, the way that lovers should,
Beckons onward through her weeping oaks,
Numbered red, the mark of their fate,

For now they await the coming steely axe,
For you dear friends, it looks to be too late.

And heavy this July bears your humid heat
Brings a salted sweat from my brow
As hard in breath, I toil up from her mouth
Where her soils so sticky, her soils so deep,
Hang her dainties enticingly along my way,
Caressing my warm and blushing cheeks,
How hard it was for Eve.

I strayed and stayed a tempted woman,
Gorging the delights, and did receive
As they greedy fed, greedily on me,
Within her woods, those humid heights,
I felt not the midges' many prickled bites
As my bare arms reached so bountiful
Far up into those cherrywood trees.

Upon my fill she let me out to fairer lands,
Leaving me stung with a departure in fragrance,
As greeted me the meadowsweets busy hums,
I broke her blossoms with my stained red hands,
Enlightened my spirit as I went forth in a trance,
Onward gaily to the dusty roads of Dymock.

Pass Me Your Torch

Pass me your torch one thousand nine hundred & ten,
And I will take it, two thousand & ten.

Abercrombie you did not know me,
But I have known you;
Now discovered all your poetries,
You, and your fine band of men.

My dreams and passion
Have ignited, riding free once again
To the cause of poetry, in my pen
For a land I love dearly.·
Born known, pulls me a poet's heart true,
One language ours speaks words
Views all, we with eyes clearly.

Friends of Dymock - a friend of poets,
Pass me your torch, dear brothers
Forever bright bums your flame,
A beacon upon the land, no end,
Where words are sweet for others,
My first love, this poem to you I send.

This is my answer to the poets of Dymock, whom I came
upon in a Tewkesbury bookshop. Dymock, familiar from a
distance, for me was undiscovered, until now. Poetry is my
first love, but they, this band of men, ignited my poetry to
further heights. My feeling is of oneness with them, that we
all share the same hearts, and passion for poetry. I wanted
to join them in this same place of Dymock, and I did, in
the next century, a hundred years later, within this land of
green England.

LOST IN THE WOODS

OCTOBER 2010

There are many woods in the forest for me to yet discover; I wonder how long it will take me to see them all. For the rest of my life, as long as I am still fit, I will ramble these woods freely, writing for you all about these beautiful places. They are your forests, rightfully yours to cherish and keep for your children.

I do hope dearly in my heart, because my heart has been troubled recently, that I am not leaving behind a distant memory of mine to you. If this fair land of woods is ever threatened, you must guard her with your life. We owe it to our future children, for she is theirs to manage, respect, and enjoy.

We have the god-given right to refresh our souls, freely reaching deep down back to their roots, which none of us should ever turn our backs on.

The long winding road from Rockfield to Monmouth takes us along the B4233, where a little pull-in with a barrier across leads down into the woods at Hendre. Drivers of woodland vehicles that manage the forest hold keys to the barrier, but people walking on foot may enter the woods by the side turn.

There is just enough room for my truck to park up close to an overhang of trees while we go a-rambling for the day. It is a dark place here with the dominant presence of a grey stone house which looks as if it has just jumped out of a fairytale. The strange building with architecture to match, of a time long past, is fast decaying. The windows and the oak front door are arched in stone, with small stone steps leading up to the door, covered generously in moss. No foot has trod here for many a year.

While we are changing our boots a woodman's truck pulls up to open the barrier; he has a full load of logs. We have a woodburner ourselves, and the back of my truck is empty. As the woodman looks at us we ask him if he would sell us his load, and he obliges. He kindly helps us load up the logs to our truck, telling us that they had been destined for Abergavenny. Looks like we were in the right place at the right time.

Charlie pays the woodman and we set off down into the forest. The long path has been well used and gravelled and has been pressed down hard by the heavy trucks.

The sky this fine morning is blue, not a cloud on the horizon, with low warm sunshine that startles the eyes, the rays of light peeping through the trees' fiery colours of autumn. A family of six jays squabble among themselves amidst the mature tree tops. I squint high up towards the racket above, sometimes getting a glimpse of the pink feather colours when they hop madly on to the lower branches. The sharp sting of autumn warns us of its presence, while the wet dewy earth scents rise up from the mulched forest floor. There is a mist in the air as the sun warms the mulch in the early part of the day.

At most times it is off the beaten track where I discover relics of humanity and hidden treasures of the plant, fungus and tree kind. Deeper foraging reveals the delightful presence of insects and animals. Sunlight penetrates the silken threads of spider ropes as they hang from branches swaying in gentle breeze. The rutting echo of the male deer penetrates the forest's silence, becoming closer and closer as we walk down between the tall flood of oaks.

A thrush sings joyfully, facing his speckled breast proudly from the tallest conifer and performing his merry tunes to all in the warmth of the morning. Blackbirds are firmly making arrangements between each other, and small birds such as tree creepers, wrens, warblers and blue tits teeter and trot about like little stars, hunting under cover in the darker parts of the forest for insects. More jays are present in the tall oaks above, and you can see them jumping from tree to tree making a racket. Through the yellow autumn colours of the oaks high up, two buzzards on patrol can be seen soaring the tree tops. This is what is irritating the jays.

As you walk down on the track road through there is a group of oaks, looking very grand and mature; they must be of great age, and have grown very close to each other. Residing underneath these oaks is a little forest gem from yesteryear of the people kind, and I do not have to go off the beaten track to get it; it just falls into my camera lens, framed in a yellow sea of oaks. This wooden wheeled object looks as if it would have been used by foresters to shelter in upon resting periods, when working the different locations around the forest. The wheels bear the manufacturer's name.

Not far ahead this track forks into three, one way leading right down by the oaks, one up to the left and around and one straight down through a clearing ahead. We choose the straight down route, where the forest floor is steep on a decline, and deeply tufty and spongy to the foot. On each side of us stand avenues of conifers. This area has been cleared at some time, for parts of the ground are boggy, due to the lack of tree roots sucking up the water.

Charlie walks on ahead while I close my eyes and dream away my senses to the scents and calls of these woods. Upon opening my eyes, I see him down on his knees. Is he praying? I did not want to disturb him, but I found that he had fallen down a rabbit hole, reducing him to knee height. He was not harmed, and we saw the funny side of it.

We decided to take the higher ground up through the woodland by Calling Wood, to see if we could get a better view over the tops of these conifers. The red soil through Calling Wood was very wet, and a little stream trickled down between our feet. The slope was tiresome, as it was two steps forward and ten steps back. Nearby there was a brackened area of past-felled conifers, covered in deep moss, which got us to the top of the wood more quickly.

Along the way up into the darkness, which was scary and shivery cold, I started thinking to myself, my imagination playing on my mind - I hope there is no mad hermit living here. A silly thought, but then most people don't venture off the track. It is amazing to think what could grow in these conditions of near blackness. Then from out of the black beamed out like beacons a family of mushrooms, grey-white and smooth, like a set of crockery plates, all in a line. They ranged from grandad and daddy size to mummy, children and baby size, and here they were growing out of the darkness, quite fairytale like. These mushrooms are called scaly tricholoma, and they grow under conifers (pines) in late autumn.

Arriving out of the wood and out into the light, breathless and sweaty, we found a log to sit on for a well-deserved flask of tea and a sandwich. The view was amazing; we could see over the treetops to a grand mansion, far in the distance - Raglan Lodge, maybe. A little way down the slope we could see blocks dotted around the grass, and Charlie said he thought they were blocks of salt for the deer.

Finishing lunch, we made our way to Telltale Wood. Through the woods we could hear the buzz of chainsaws and men at work, but we could not see them. Further into the woods were two old grabbing machines left growing with the shrubbery, looking as if they had not been used for years. There were oil drums strewn around, and it smelled of oil and diesel everywhere. The foresters might have had to chainsaw their way out of this one, when they wanted the machines for scrap or the museum.

Out of the woods, on to the regular track road within the forest where the log lorries had travelled, trees had been cut and stacked alongside the forest road that wound up into other woods ahead. The chainsaws echoed through the afternoon, and we came across a large pile of wood, which had not been chopped up long as it gave a creamy damp aroma of freshness. A stone's throw away from the woodpile was a stand of chestnut trees which were already ripe and had given up their bounty. We kicked about the autumn leaves to reveal the chestnuts split open from their prickly shells. I had not seen chestnuts this large for years.

We filled our pockets greedily, and then the itching began. Midges were biting aplenty in this part of the woods, I could feel the pinpricks under my hairline and neck. It got to the stage where I had to retreat to the track. Remembering that my mate Mike had given me an army mosquito net to wear on my forest adventures, I put the net over my head. Foiled again midges! It worked, but no kidding, I scratched for a week after this walk.

When we had left the chestnuts behind we rearranged the woodman's log pile for a laugh, building strange things with the logs.

It would soon get dark, and we knew we should be

returning home, as it was 4pm already. It is all very well looking forward to new adventures, but the time runs away quickly when you are busy discovering. We had been six hours walking now, so it would be a bit of a march back to the truck.

Stupidly, instead of returning on the lorry track home, we got lost and took a wrong turn. Slogging on for over an hour, and worrying about nightfall added to the panic, and I was beginning to lose it a bit. But suddenly as we neared the track road, we heard the big roar of a lorry engine and the clanking of a grabbing hydraulic loading cut trees from the side road. Yes, we were back where we had started from by the woodpile. We felt so stupid.

For a while, we watched the forester load up his lorry and I took photographs of him working. Upon returning to the road, it seemed we were walking forever. We were tired and worn out and the fun had gone out of it a bit. Light was fading fast, and we began to hear the screeches of owls, creatures of the night. I got them to answer back, as for years I have been mastering their calls. I seem to fool them with my human voice, and it works every time.

The heavy forestry lorry passed us by, and I thought, if only we could get a lift off him, but we kept walking. In the distance of the woods we could see lamp lights moving about in the dusk. It looked scary, but that's how your body gets at night. I just assumed these people were coming out to hunt at nightfall.

When we at last got back to the truck in the pitch black, we could not see a thing. The truck waiting under the bushes looked so inviting, as was the damp and woody aroma from the logs in back. The forest scents followed us as we drove, satisfied, tired and hungry, back home, and those logs from the woodman did keep us kindly warm. When the flames licked around a log through the glass in the woodburner we were there again, deep in the forest of Hendre.

THREE MAGICAL WOODLANDS

NOVEMBER 2010

November is beginning to show its presence by the sharp sting in the air against our faces, and fresh earthy scents rise up from the moist brackens of wet logs, moss and ferns as the distant sun streaks through the trees, casting warmth to the cold forest floor. Everywhere is bronze and gold, all on fire, displaying a last farewell until next spring. The sun burns amber in the true blue sky, casting beams of light across the land, low and blinding to look at.

The small road with a white barrier gate forks into two paths. One is the regular path, out under a railway bridge to the main road, and the other is a path made by machines which lead up into secluded forest. The steep difficult incline up through the woods is a breathtaking effort, and I have to keep stopping. The forest ground has been heavily machined through, as large track wheels have indented the soft watered wooded area into Bonds Wood.

With great difficulty Charlie and I master climbing up

this incline and into the craters the big wheels have left behind. To get through the woods to the top is a challenge, but it is worth it to find out where it leads to next. Eventually we find a path at the top which looks hidden and unused. Along the same path the other way there are about five cottages, some of them run down and just lived in.

All is quiet and no one is about, which gives us the feeling that we are trespassing on people's land. I cannot stop looking as I think to myself people must live here, because, unkempt and dilapidated as the properties look, the workings of self-sufficient living are present and recent. One cottage has a large people-carrier in the drive, which makes us wonder how it got there and where can it go from this point.

Carrying on deeper through the woods, the forest path has been turfed up and is a mess; the damage is recent, so it must have been done the night before by animals. We come to one more cottage deeper into the woods, well kept and with a pretty garden. It has large iron gates to cordon the property off from the main woods. The ground up to these gates appears to have been bulldozed by a herd of wild boar – it looks like a ploughed field. I don't think deer would have made such a mess, they are too delicate. Perhaps the boar were looking for worms and truffles in the dark of the night, and that's why the gate is there; without it these people would not have a garden left.

I am amused to think that living so deep in the forest when it is pitch black it must be quite scary to hear the boars in great numbers so close, snuffling and grunting about by the house. A man told me once that at White Rocks Woods his wife had a garden full of tulips, until the deer discovered them and ate the lot in one night, so he had to cordon the garden off from the woods. So if you live in the woods, and I have seen it often, you have to protect the flowers and vegetables from the night creatures.

Walking on through to Birchen Wood, there is a slight incline again up to the top edge, where you can look out towards buckstone and farmland. Over towards the farm are softly heard the distant cries of sheep and farm life, the only sounds that pierce the still airs. Coming through Knockalls Enclosure and down to Bunjups Wood, it appears dark and moisture starved to the enclosed closely-knitted short conifers. Chestnut trees further on the way tower and hang over the path below and have dropped all their fare of chestnuts to the boggy forest path, much to the delight of Charlie, who fills his pockets up with them. We stop for a late lunch, as our tummies are grumbling, and some old logs that have been felled a long time ago lie wet and green, so Charlie offers his coat for me to sit on. A flask of tea with cheese and onion sandwiches makes a welcome break in the darkening day in Bunjups Wood. Robins flit out of the shrubbery and are happy to come up close and share our crumbs.

Dusk is calling as the night is drawing in, and quickly we hurry up the walk from the wood, as time can tend to be forgotten. The route down leads us back to the white barrier gate we were at earlier. Close by this gate is a small concrete road to the main road, with a brook running alongside it. This brook runs through much land from afar and is sadly getting blocked by the domestic rubbish of lazy people. A few old washing machines, a rusty fridge and even more stuff have been dumped further on, blocking the flow of the water.

Along this single road we come to a disused railway bridge, the low sun shining in all the right places this late Sunday afternoon to show the structure off at its finest. The skill and workmanship used to produce this wonderful piece of history display the highest standards of creativity, and I'm sure has long disappeared. The cost of producing this kind of work would now be too high, and the skills to build it hard to match. It would be a dreadful shame for the forest to lose this bridge, and the many others. For what once was, with all its beginnings, we need to keep these gems together for our future generations, for our heritage, for historical and educational purposes, of our past working lives in the forest.

CHEERING FOR OUR BOYS

DECEMBER 2010

Early in December 2010 the hard weather had kept the country captive in ice, and there were no signs of a thaw showing yet. It was lethal to walk the pavements, even in the towns where it might have been warmer with the buildings.

The M50 from Tewkesbury was warmer from the traffic flow and free from ice, so clear roads were ours. We had made arrangements to pick some wood up again at Hendre Monmouth, and we were going to meet our old friend the woodman at the wood's gate. The morning became brighter still with the blue skies appearing fast, and the sun soon burned away the fog and mists of the early morning.

We arrived at the wood's entrance and waited a while, until our friend pulled in to greet us with his load of wood. We had a good conversation together while he helped us load up the wood into our truck from his, and the talk was something to do with outside privys and no bathrooms, which we all knew about once when we were children, as the woodman was about our age. Charlie and I thanked him for the logs, and when we were done loading we paid him and bid him farewell until the next time, which would be soon enough as these woodburners do eat the logs up fast.

Wanting to make more of a day of it, because it's a good forty miles from Tewkesbury, we came to Monmouth town by Monnow Bridge. Our truck was right up to the front seats and full to the brim with the damp sweating wood, and no doubt many forest bugs. We had locked the truck up when we noticed that there was a hive of activity around Monnow Bridge. Troops were getting out of army trucks and mobilising, and this did alarm me, because I knew nothing of the parade that was due to happen in the town. I thought something major had happened, like an act of terrorism, and that the army had been called in. I then realised that the Monmouthshire Royal Engineers had not long come back home from a tour of duty in Afghanistan. Soldiers were marching from the old bridge through the town, then on to take a salute at the shire hall. After this they would all arrive at St Mary's Parish Church for thanksgiving, and medals would be issued to the soldiers for their service in Afghanistan.

As we both stood on the old Monnow Bridge, all the military assembled. The brass band was playing and leading the troops, and it was a sight to see, I felt extremely proud and emotional. We were in a good position, in a dip on the bridge looking on to the troops as they marched over towards us, and my camera was at the ready when they came over the top. When the band and troops had passed by I was aware of a foreign-looking man standing close by me, with a uniform of a different colour, and many medals attached to his jacket. He looked very important. I was itching to ask him for a photograph, but I felt shy, even though Charlie kept saying, go on it will be OK, ask him for a photo. I did not, because I thought it might be disrespectful to ask him on this special day. I'm just not cheeky enough to do it, and I regretted it for ages afterwards.

By the time we had reached the shire hall at the top of the town, most of the soldiers and dignitaries had entered St Mary's Church for the service. The media were there, and so were two gentlemen standing outside the church gates in full uniform, both with lots of medals. The gentleman I had seen earlier on Monnow Bridge was one of them and he shook hands with the black gentleman, again in a different coloured uniform, with many medals. We stood about four feet away from them, but with the buzz of media activity around them I felt awkward to ask for a photograph. Now I greatly regret that I did not ask.

Anyway this day was unexpected, as we knew nothing of the Monmouthshire Royal Engineers' visit and it was a nice surprise. At least I have a story to tell. We were there in the thick of it, and I got my photographs of what was most important - these men who lay down their lives for others.

Later in the following year there was a television programme called Police Academy UK, in which I recognised the two gentlemen we had twice seen that day standing outside St Mary's Church. I realised that they had been part of a television programme, working alongside the British police. Now I felt even more annoyed with myself for not getting that photograph, but not for long as I have my other photographs, of the dear men who are 'Our Boys'.

FERNEYHOUGH FOUNDATIONS

2011

A little story was found within the Ferneyhough family into which I married. It was a proud story to possess for them all, and it was brought up quite often in our family conversations.

The story should have its proper place in Wales. This event occurred in the mid 1960s, and Lenny, my husband's eldest brother, was in attendance at a secondary school in Gloucester at the time. He was about fifteen years old, and was chosen from many pupils to go to the forest to camp for a week. The week would include the contributions of hard work from the lucky chosen pupils, as they would all be taking part in preparing the building foundations of the Biblins Youth Hostel, in the Forest of Dean.

This large wooden hut by the River Wye would one day soon house young people from all over the country, and later the world. This has now been done for decades, enabling young people to enjoy canoeing and camping and stay within the forest.

Lenny came here with his school as a young boy and camped here at Biblins one winter in the mid 1960s. The tents then were made of thick canvas, pegged and roped to the ground, with a piece of plastic for a ground sheet. Blankets from home were all the lads had to wrap up in to keep warm at night. They had none of the luxuries we have today, with cosy sleeping bags and draught-proof tents. Their tents were pegged out in a circle, with a fire in the middle for warmth and cooking.

The work in the day for the building foundations was quite a labour-intensive project, as the mixing of concrete, shovelling and levelling was a big team job for the boys. It was all supervised and gave the boys a sense of achievement in putting their stamp on the Biblins building. This would have been enough to make a man out of these schoolboys, and it certainly did, as Lenny related to us.

It can be cold at the best of times down by the Wye, and in the winter the winds can chill you to the bone, specially when they come down along the river like a tunnel draught. But the boys were willing and had the young blood and the guts to get the job done. Later on, when it was time to retire for grub and rest, they would huddle around the campfire, grilling their delights of campfire cuisine, sausages and beans.

One night it got pretty cold, and the teachers gave out extra blankets to the boys. The cold was rising up from the frozen ground, and inside the boys' tents the warmth of more blankets and body heat made no difference, as the weather was about to take a turn for the worse. The gap between their tents and the ground made it harder to keep warm, as the draught came under and through. That night the snow fell heavily, so heavily that as the night wore on it was not possible to stay here in these raw conditions. In the end the boys and the teachers were completely snowed in. Lenny said the snow was up past their knees.

My mother-in-law Mary told me she had had the radio on while washing up at the sink, and was thinking about her son out in these changing elements, not realising how bad it had got up at Biblins. It was soon broadcast on the radio that the army had been called out into the forest to bail out schoolboys and teachers from the near-Arctic conditions.

Lenny said as they all waited to be rescued, the army arrived in their Ford three-ton open-backed lorries. They had taken the route along the bottom road, the other side of the river, and the boys had to walk the swing bridge to the soldiers waiting on the other side. Lenny said they were all relieved and elated by the excitement of being rescued by the army.

Heavy snow continued to fall upon them as they crossed Biblins Bridge a few at a time. This was all that could be allowed, as the bridge was not secured as well as it is today, and it must have had quite a swing on it, with the hurrying boys crossing the river up so high to get into a real army truck. I'm sure the excitement of this all was an experience never to be forgotten, and may have even tempted some of the boys into an army career later on. It must have been like an army training course, with conditions to match. From the glee in my brother- in -laws eyes when he tells us his story, I bet the boys would not have had it any other way.

So you see this story is a family affair, with the contributions from Lenny and his old school chums, in the building of Biblins. And for the Ferneyhough family, Lenny has proudly put his stamp on South Wales as the Ferneyhough foundations.

DYMOCK GOLD

MARCH 2011

I am a firm believer in connecting with the past, and this I do through my happy world of poetry. The forest and all she has to give were set in stone for me in that happy land of Dymock. Once you meet her she casts her spell on you, never to be the same again. Bliss!

I arrived in Dymock a hundred years later, when spring was in full pursuit, and the poets of the past called me here to share in their connection. Back in 2010, I stumbled upon the Dymock poets in a Tewkesbury bookshop, in the poetry section. This book jumped out at me. It had an attractive green cover, with an old photograph of four men, all in clothes from the 1900s. I began to take a deep interest in these men and their lives. A deep connection developed, as I knew that we had the same passion for poetry and nature. We were generations apart, but we had the same hearts wrapped in poetry.

My camera battery was charged full as I waited with butterflies in my tummy for the coming delights, of a sight I had never seen before; the great multitude of wild daffodils called 'Dymock Gold'.

Mother came with us on this trip. She was 82 and looking forward to a trip down Memory Lane. Boots, gaiters, sticks, warm coats, a flask of tea and lunch were packed in my truck. We turned off the M50 at Newent and took the B4215 to Oxenhall. The small dusty road had a warm cosy feeling about it as the newness of spring emerged from tree, bush, hedge and verge. This new birth awakened our spirits from the long slumber and gripping wilderness of the winter past.

On our way through the dusty lanes to Oxenhall, I remember seeing through the hedge a small field at a slope, riding down from a wooded area. This parcel of land was full to the brim with strange, multi-coloured primroses. There were some of the common natural yellow type mingled with them. My thoughts were that if those cultivated primroses had been introduced among the naturals in the past, they had multiplied naturally in this small pocket of land. It was a spectacular display.

We slowly passed by Oxenhall Church and approached St Anne's Vineyard. At the entrance of a very old black and white cottage, we parked the truck off the narrow road. The hedges along to the cottage gate were caressed by a tangle of delicate white blossoms, and behind the hedge was a coarse grass field, where spring lambs played happily with each other. Those bouncy woolly babes were jumping around at each other and roaming around in their packs, looking for the next thing that moved. The ewes were busy chewing the grass, and were not much amused by the children's jolly antics.

Mother was stuck in the back seat of my truck, because

it has only two doors and the seat has to be pulled forward. Getting her in was a game, but getting her out was a joke. While wrestling with a pull and a lean on to me, it was nearly a piggyback for mother, until she landed eventually on the firm ground.

The gravel drive led up to a very pretty cottage, with gardens of traditional flowers which were yet to emerge. We entered a very small room where shelves were packed ceiling high with an amazing variety of hedgerow pickles, jams and wines, along with local cheeses. The variety of stock was amazing and it took us ages to choose. The owner seemed a little impatient with us as we all hummed and hahed. We were spoilt for choice, so Mother and I bought each other wine and Charlie chose a local whole cheese for himself. We did spend a bit of money here, leaving most happy with the bounties of this fair land.

Following up through the lanes to Dymock we passed Betty Daw's Wood, where many people were out taking a walk. We decided that lunch was to be taken soon, so we travelled the road through Dymock Woods, stopping on the way to take no end of photographs. I could not get enough of these little beauties. The woods were swathed in tides of yellow, and for me this was heaven.

We did eventually stop for lunch, when I got over my frenzy of photo madness. The truck was stopped at Murrells End, not far from the woods, and there we dined like royalty. Mother at this stage was in the front seat, as the capers of seat changing were not an option for her at her age. Our lunch consisted of thick gammon bacon, a good chunk of cheese each, a boiled egg each and doorsteps of dry bread, plus tea. A simple humble fare, but enjoyed by all as we watched out of the truck window for bird movement and held dear the stillness of the woods.

We kept the truck doors slightly open, and the air was still and fresh with the new-born scents of awakened springtime. The only sound that broke the silence of the afternoon was a horse in the distance through the woods, put away for a time in its stables. The din that animal was making echoed on through to us. All this neighing and sharp loud kicking could be heard, as its hoofs belted hard on the stable doors. After a short time, a lady rode by on a tall fine horse, putting her hand up to us with a nod of her head. The horse clopped by slowly, then turned into the woods on to the track, while this horsey din went on regardless. I think the horse in the stables knew that the other horse had been taken out, and it did not like it, hence the racket.

Finishing our lunches, Mother got out of the truck to put on her coat and collect her sticks from the boot. I was getting out to meet her when all of a sudden she looked into my eyes with great emotion, and with a tear pulled me close to her, holding me so tight I could not breathe. I was amazed at her strength, but feelings were running high for Mary, as the memories of Dymock to her were really special. The visit had brought back memories of when she was young and with her husband Len, our father.

We lost Dad in March 2008, and it was a rough old time with his illness. But many moons ago Dad and Mom were childhood sweethearts, and she told me that when they were

218

in their teens, Dad used to show off to her and her sister Ivy on his old bike. Dad's family came from Monmouth and the Ferneyhoughs lived for a time in Newent when Dad was a boy. His dad Fred Ferneyhough got work on the farms, and moving around with his work was a regular thing. Mother's mom lived at Over Bridge in Over Cottage and her mom Alice worked at the Dog Inn cleaning the floors. Mother worked at this same inn when she left school, and told me many stories about when she used to churn the butter in a large barrel, turning and turning it exhaustingly to make the inn's butter.

Mother said the road by the cottage from Gloucester to Newent was very small, and just over the road was an apple orchard with many trees. She said the gypsies that stopped by the Dog Inn were handed their beers outside the door, as they were not permitted to come inside, simply because when they drank they were always fighting.

Ivy was Mother's little sister, and they both rode out to Dymock on their bicycles in season to pick daffies, putting them in their baskets and taking them home to their mom to be sold. As a boy, Dad went with his brother Jim picking the daffies along the road, selling these sweet little gems to passing motorists, of which there were not many at this time. I can just imagine those boys with their wartime short back and sides haircuts and their grey long shorts overhanging their knobbly grazed knees, with baggy wool socks tucked into their scuffed, hobnailed and much-repaired boots. No new shoes then, big brother's were passed down to the next.

Mother tells me that when she was at school there was a gypsy girl in her class called Phoebe Baton. She remembers a time when Phoebe was not in school one day, so the teacher asked her the following day why she had been absent. Phoebe answered, 'I was daffyin, missus', to the sniggers of classmates, including Mother. Phoebe was out contributing with her family to picking daffies in Dymock from the hedgerows, because the flowers had longer stalks than those in the fields. They were collected by the Romany gypsy people in their big baskets, and they all took their Dymock daffies to Gloucester and sold them at the Cross. At this time most people did not have cars and could not get out to the country, so these rural posies from Dymock were well received by the people of the towns.

★ ★ ★ ★ ★

Getting back to Dymock Woods, we all walked our lunch off, and the horse through yonder was still neighing and kicking the stable doors. It went on for the best part of two hours. Continuing on through, some way from the regular track there was a boggy area which I tramped through; sometimes in these deeper parts of the woodland you will find undisturbed little Gardens of Eden. Attractive small grasses and mosses of different kinds and miniature ferns grew together over rocks with pockets in between. You could never create a garden like this, as nature has the upper hand on these things.

While I was getting carried away with my close-up

photographs, being mostly on my knees and in silly positions, I forgot the midges - little blighters. Later on in the day I found myself scratching wildly under my hairline.

Towards the end of the wood, great firs had been felled, and they were stacked in large rows on top of each other. The sap was bleeding out of the trunks the colour of blood, which felt to me a bit sad. We all walked back through the woods, where upon the regular track gorse bushes threw their bright fresh yellow sprays of colour at us, which was quite refreshing, as parts of the woods are still sparse and leafless. Young shoulder height beech sapling leaves were emerging from their young trunks on spindly branches as pointed brown cases unwrapped like ice cream cones. Damp earthy mists rose to the occasion from the forest floor, and there was a chill in the air as the late afternoon wore on.

★ ★ ★ ★ ★

Approaching my truck where we had left it, the dusty road out of Dymock brought us through lanes to Kempley, where verges and ditches were a confetti of long-stalked daffodils, just as the gypsies once liked them. There was a field on the way through which was beautifully paved with gold, and it was everything I ever wanted to see with our mother and Charlie. It took us all aback to see how full to the brim this field was of daffodils - they were bunched in millions and could not have grown any closer to each other.

Towards the back of the field was a tall pile of old felled

trees from past years, and mists were rising from the pile. The sky was white with cloud but bright, and the conditions of were well suited to this springtime day as I took endless photographs from the old gate of the vibrant sea of yellow gold beyond. Composing myself to some control, we were beckoned onwards to St Mary's Church at Kempley, where we were greeted by an adornment of daffodils as we walked through the gate and up the long path to the old church. These beauties of yellow gold abounded in their glory with a claim to the land, which was theirs now. The little daffies filled every flowerless grave around the churchyard, and children's graves of long ago were worn and faceless, the words long eroded away, but the overwhelming yellow blooms which filled their sleep above them gave a tiny sprinkling of gold to the purity and innocence of the children.

WANDERING THE
WINDS OF
REDBROOK

∽

OCTOBER 2011

It was October 2011, and in a few days time I was due to have my shredded knee cartilage trimmed in hospital. As I did not know how long it would be before I was walking out and working again, Charlie suggested a visit to the forest.

The day was a blustery one. To most people it would a risk to be about in high winds, when trees can come falling down in the forests, but blustery is the way I like it. There seems to be more of an attraction for me to be here in these conditions in the woods. The extreme movements of the winds catch the tree tops, making them sway and bend, and making different sounds as the winds whip through the soul of the woods. That's why feeling the elements and being at one with the forest contributes to the fascination.

The Old Church at Penallt signs us on through the lanes of Redbrook. The scattered ancient walls at one time divided up the land through these woods, perhaps for keeping animals in. The stones are boulder sized and built like stone walling, but on a larger scale. They are shaped to fit well, making proper divides. They are covered in rich green mosses, from decades of good forest moisture. Some have collapsed and rolled away into the undergrowth. Standing crooked in places are massive stone gateposts five or six feet in height, making gateways in the former walls to the portioned-off land. Men once worked in these woods with their horses, shifting sawn and chopped trees all day. Working the landscape for wages and food, a simple but hard way of life, must have been an extreme task. There was no technology, just the animals they lived with and relied on to survive. Oil is our technology, and what, I wonder, will we leave behind because of it? But there are too many of us now to go back, even if we had to.

Carrying on down the lane to the Boat Inn, the little old chimney is smoking a warm wood fire, sending the sweet scents of the forest to our noses. Our dear friend Jim, master beekeeper of the forest, stands on the balcony, looking out to the river with his glass of red wine. I always like to stand outside and look out over the river to talk with Jim. He is pleased to see us, and we have lots of laughs with him. He talks of such an interesting past. His favourite saying, in that mischievous tone and with a cheeky look in his eye, is "I'm just a simple country boy". I love him to bits, he's the cutest man I have ever met.

Later in the afternoon, Jim tells us a story. When he was twelve, in the war, he remembers when ammunition was being carried across the railway viaduct. One of the mules carrying this load fell between the slim footing on the railway viaduct, and nearly fell through into the river below. The animal was spared only because the load got caught each side of it. Jim said it had been a bit of a game to get the animal up and mobile again, with its dangerous load. The conversation went on into the afternoon, about men working with horses and how Jim himself, when he was younger, had worked in the woods with horses. He told us that these had been some of the best years of his life.

In the afternoon we all departed our ways soon enough, as the day was getting on. We drove on toward the end of Lone Lane, where there is a pull in, with iron gates. Charlie said to me, "Are you up for a last walk?" I replied that there was still some light in the day and said "Yes, let's do it". I did not intend to walk far, as my shredded cartilage was getting painful to bear weight on.

We got out of the truck to be almost bowled over by the winds, which had now become wild. Dark clouds were forming, so I guessed this walk would be short. A lady walked by us with her dogs, concerned that we were trying to cross the gate to her father's place. We assured her that we were taking a walk across the fields, and asked if could we leave our truck there. She said that was OK, but asked us not to block the entrance. She told us that the fields were a nice walk, but we would have to jump a few stone stiles. She also told us that this land was being bought by the TV presenter Kate Humble, and a lot of people were not happy about it. I thought that if she cared about wildlife she should be the right person to own it, and I hope she lives up to that.

As we walked through the thick swaying grass to each field, there were ancient divides between them all. They were man made from flat heavy rock, and each one was different. I took photos of both sides of the stiles, because the handiwork was different in shape on both sides. The past here is so evident, and so lasting, and because Redbrook retains the past so well, you really feel transported back in time. The field we stood in was full from end to end with the thistle-like flowers of common knapweed, flowering from July to September. They were all over now, but a month ago this field would have been a colourful picture. Next year I will be here and own that picture, I thought.

Looking down by my feet into the deep, thick grass, I saw that the grass was pressed flat, as if an animal such as a deer had been sleeping here the night before. To the back of me, as I looked around, was a stone wall with barbed wire on top. I peeked over the wall to find a view to die for. As I looked down into grazing fields far into the distance, the fields dipped deep, forging ahead to rich land. The land raced away with my amazed eyes, up and over to yonder wherever. Pine trees dominated the backdrop of my picture postcard, with miles of forest. I didn't expect such a view over that wall.

We walked four fields, lifting our tired legs and sore knees a thousand times over meadow-rich grasses, boggy in most areas. Oaks of good age around these fields grow strong and dominant. Old roads or tracks are still evident around these overgrown fields, with twisted oaks in strange shapes competing for light and space, growing untidily in the fast-disappearing tracks. Be they drover tracks or farmworkers' tracks, they are evidence of times past.

THE OAKS' GRAVEYARD

∽

NEW YEAR'S EVE 2011

Christmas is over, and today is New Year's Eve. It was my desire to get to Dymock before 2011 was out, as there was a very important reason for me, as a poet, to be in Dymock. I remember in springtime visiting Dymock Woods for the first time. Upon seeing her divine English yellow beauties of springtime, I really thought I had died and gone to heaven; hence the poem "Jewel in the Crown of Dymock" was born.

But today my reason to visit Dymock is that one hundred years ago, in 1911, Lascelles Abercrombie moved there. Not that I am ranking myself with these great poets, but I do share their passion for poetry with the world around us as we express the deep need to pour out the soul.

Here I am with my husband Charlie, driving the shady roads through Dymock Woods. How different she looks today. On this last day of 2011 the sun is low and slightly warm, and the air is forever earthy and fresh. With the last special day of this part of the century the sky is a traditional true blue. Arriving at the foot of these woods just off the road, we pull in where we ate our humble lunch with mother in the springtime. There came to me a sight unexpected and sad. Beyond the locked gate to the woods, our eyes were met by a graveyard of oaks. The path into the woods loomed large with tidy oaks lying side by side, all felled and numbered and ready to go. Go where? I thought, my mind feeling the loss at all the years those oaks had been growing in Dymock Woods, and well before Abercrombie, Thomas and Gibson. All good things have to come to an end, including all the good poets.

For all the seasons felt and lived by these oaks, through at least 150 years, I prayed please God, let them not go abroad, please let them stay in England. They came from our soils for proper English houses.

Charlie counted the rings on one tree, and it was not the largest. One hundred and thirty years old, the rings told us. These oaks were all numbered on their trunk ends, and the oak tree stored closest to the gate entrance was numbered 49. I do not know if that means 49 oaks were felled in these woods alone, as I cannot imagine that so many oaks would be available here. Further on were stacked trunks of pine and beech, so maybe that was the number of all the trees felled in these woods this year.

My daughter has a friend called Tom who is very good at carpentry. She suggested that I should collect some small pieces of oak lying around the forest and bring them home, so that Tom could make something small with them for me, as a good English gift from the heart of Dymock Woods. It was a good idea, a little family heirloom perhaps, to pass on from poets' land.

Oaks were now lying in state on the pathway out, dragged out from the roots of their birth, so it was a graveyard indeed. But all the living they had done had ended in useful purpose. With their enormous size, on their backs against the forest floor, I still felt tearful at their horizontal state. But this is woodland management, and the great oaks were now mature enough to be used. I took photographs, but felt that Dymock had nurtured these beautiful trees in her bosom, and it felt to me like a mother giving up her children.

Dymock Church was our next port of call, and I was not disappointed. The church grounds are surrounded by some of the oldest residents, and the graveyard headstones and family vaults feature the work of some of the most talented stone workers of the time. As an undertaker's daughter myself, being born into an old-established family in Tewkesbury, and coming from a long line of undertakers since the early 1800s, this little old community fascinated me; it was in my blood. I looked around me at where these folk of ages past were born, educated, worked and died, to lie now in their resting places, back in the Dymock earth.

This was December 31st and snowdrops were gathered in great number among a cluster of gravestones. A mat of white, with strong stems and leaves and big bell flowers, tinkled their snow-white heads in the keen wind. A couple passing by told me that the snowdrops were there every year, but this was the first time they had emerged so early. As the keen winds blew overhead cones fell and scattered about me, shed by a giant fir within the church grounds. A few yew trees old and ancient, gnarled and twisty, darkened our path to the church door.

The church is a beautiful design in red stone, which in most parts is fast fading away from the effects of our dirty world, acid rain making the stone flake off in chunks. Inside the porch are displayed the names of people from the past who contributed money to their community and the poor. The church is a fine place of worship and looks rich in activity; you can see it is greatly loved by the community. The poets' corner I have enjoyed and further learned from and left my message.

Jewel in the crown of Dymock

Golden golden delights,
That mine eyes do see
Her millions quiver abundant yonder
In mid-March breezes
Thy sight is blinded with her teases,
Celestial lights brought from heaven.

Brightest as the new morning star
Through the lanes of Kempley

To the old church that stands
Surround in abound, St Mary's
Full to the brim wide and far.
Fair maidens these golden beauties
Swell to the great ebb of yellow sea,
And yet, like the fullness of a swollen bore,
Seeking further refuge in her red soils.
Ah...sweet red cloddy earth.

Upon her past times
Gatherers of the season hard toiled,
From long ago those days of olden
When the cloth sang to the joys
Of the bounties of Dymock.
Ah... golden, so golden.

Written March 2011 from memory, in Dymock, (at
Pendock, while about my day work) .

Upon returning home, it was nice of Charlie to drive me around for the day and stop by the Old Nailshop, where Wilfred Gibson lived with his family. It is wonderful to know that the Dymock Poets were all here together and sat in this abode, gathered in good conversation at this cottage in the month of July 1914. My favourite piece by Wilfred Gibson is *The Golden Room*; it says it all about those wonderful men who were our Dymock poets. I am going to finish this book by quoting you part of it

Do you remember the still summer evening
When in the cosy cream-washed living-room
Of the Old Nailshop we all talked and laughed
Our neighbors from the Gallows, Catherine
And Lascelles Abercrombie; Rupert Brooke;
Eleanor and Robert Frost, living awhile
At Little Iddens, who'd brought over with them
Helen and Edward Thomas? In the lamplight
We talked and laughed, but for the most part listened

While Robert Frost kept on and on and on
In his slow New England fashion for our delight,
Holding us with shrewd turns and racy quips,
And the rare twinkle of his grave blue eyes.

We sat there in the lamplight while the day
Died from rose-latticed casements, and the plovers
Called over the low meadows till the owls
Answered them from the elms; we sat and talked
Now a quick flash from Abercrombie, now
A murmured dry half-heard aside from Thomas,
Now a clear laughing word from Brooke, and then
Again Frost's rich and ripe philosophy
That had the body and tang of good draught cider
And poured as clear a stream.

- from The Golden Room, Wilfred Gibson